THE FIRST STEP ACT OF 2018:

A Reformatted And Easy To Read Pocket Guide

© 2019 Federal Sentencing Alliance
www.FederalSentencingAlliance.com

Introduction

The First Step Act Of 2018 was signed into law on December 21, 2018 and is presently *on the cusp* of the implementation phase that will be ongoing from January 15, 2020 through January 15, 2022.

Many are trying to understand the Act and find it hard to read in it's published form online.

This book is a recitation of the First Step Act Of 2018 in a reformatted, easy to read version, size 14 font, and with all sub-paragraphs indented for context.

There is *no analysis included in this book*, just the First Step Act Of 2018, as reformatted.

Federal Sentencing Alliance has authored *other First Step Act Of 2018 publications* analyzing various provisions of the Act in an effort to foster learning of substantive provisions thereof, by showing how specific provisions of the Act might apply in any given case.

This publication only contains the First Step Act Of 2018 as reformatted for ease of reading, and contains 214 pages of liberally spaced, size 14 font text, as reformatted.

S. 756 - First Step Act of 2018
115th Congress (2017-2018)
Second Session

Begun and held at the City of Washington on Wednesday, the third day of January, two thousand and eighteen-

To reauthorize and amend the Marine Debris Act to promote international action to reduce marine debris, and for other purposes.

Be it enacted by the Senate and House of Representatives of the United States of America in Congress assembled,

SECTION 1. Short title; table of contents.

(a) Short title.-This Act may be cited as the **First Step Act of 2018**.

(b) Table of contents.-The table of contents for this Act is as follows:

Sec. 1. Short title; table of contents.

TITLE I RECIDIVISM REDUCTION

Sec. 101. Risk and needs assessment system.
Sec. 102. Implementation of system and recommendations by Bureau of Prisons.
Sec. 103. GAO report.
Sec. 104. Authorization of appropriations.
Sec. 105. Rule of construction.
Sec. 106. Faith-based considerations.
Sec. 107. Independent Review Committee.

TITLE II BUREAU OF PRISONS SECURE FIREARMS STORAGE

Sec. 201. Short title.
Sec. 202. Secure firearms storage.

TITLE III RESTRAINTS ON PREGNANT PRISONERS PROHIBITED

Sec. 301. Use of restraints on prisoners during the period of pregnancy and postpartum recovery prohibited.

TITLE IV SENTENCING REFORM

Sec. 401. Reduce and restrict enhanced sentencing for prior drug felonies.
Sec. 402. Broadening of existing safety valve.
Sec. 403. Clarification of section 924(c) of title 18, United States Code.
Sec. 404. Application of Fair Sentencing Act.

TITLE V SECOND CHANCE ACT OF 2007 REAUTHORIZATION

Sec. 501. Short title.
Sec. 502. Improvements to existing programs.
Sec. 503. Audit and accountability of grantees.
Sec. 504. Federal reentry improvements.
Sec. 505. Federal interagency reentry coordination.
Sec. 506. Conference expenditures.
Sec. 507. Evaluation of the Second Chance Act program.
Sec. 508. GAO review.

TITLE VI MISCELLANEOUS CRIMINAL JUSTICE

Sec. 601. Placement of prisoners close to families.
Sec. 602. Home confinement for low-risk prisoners.
Sec. 603. Federal prisoner reentry initiative reauthorization; modification of imposed term of imprisonment.
Sec. 604. Identification for returning citizens.
Sec. 605. Expanding inmate employment through Federal Prison Industries.
Sec. 606. De-escalation training.
Sec. 607. Evidence-Based treatment for opioid and heroin abuse.
Sec. 608. Pilot programs.
Sec. 609. Ensuring supervision of released sexually dangerous persons.
Sec. 610. Data collection.
Sec. 611. Healthcare products.
Sec. 612. Adult and juvenile collaboration programs.
Sec. 613. Juvenile solitary confinement.

TITLE I Recidivism reduction

SEC. 101. Risk and needs assessment system.

(a) In general.-Chapter 229 of title 18, United States Code, is amended by inserting after subchapter C the following:

SUBCHAPTER D-RISK AND NEEDS ASSESSMENT SYSTEM

Sec.
3631. Duties of the Attorney General.
3632. Development of risk and needs assessment system.
3633. Evidence-based recidivism reduction program and recommendations.
3634. Report.
3635. Definitions.

§ 3631. Duties of the Attorney General

(a) In general.-The Attorney General shall carry out this subchapter in consultation with-

(1) the Director of the Bureau of Prisons;

(2) the Director of the Administrative Office of the United States Courts;

(3) the Director of the Office of Probation and Pretrial Services;

(4) the Director of the National Institute of Justice;

(5) the Director of the National Institute of Corrections; and

(6) the Independent Review Committee authorized by the First Step Act of 2018.

(b) Duties.-The Attorney General shall-

(1) conduct a review of the existing prisoner risk and needs assessment systems in operation on the date of enactment of this subchapter;

(2) develop recommendations regarding evidence-based recidivism reduction

programs and productive activities in accordance with section 3633;

   (3) conduct ongoing research and data analysis on-

    (A) evidence-based recidivism reduction programs relating to the use of prisoner risk and needs assessment tools;

    (B) the most effective and efficient uses of such programs;

    (C) which evidence-based recidivism reduction programs are the most effective at reducing recidivism, and the type, amount, and intensity of programming that most effectively reduces the risk of recidivism; and

    (D) products purchased by Federal agencies that are manufactured overseas and could be manufactured by prisoners participating in a prison work program without reducing job opportunities for other workers in the United States;

(4) on an annual basis, review, validate, and release publicly on the Department of Justice website the risk and needs assessment system, which review shall include-

(A) any subsequent changes to the risk and needs assessment system made after the date of enactment of this subchapter;

(B) the recommendations developed under paragraph (2), using the research conducted under paragraph (3);

(C) an evaluation to ensure that the risk and needs assessment system bases the assessment of each prisoner's risk of recidivism on indicators of progress and of regression that are dynamic and that can reasonably be expected to change while in prison;

(D) statistical validation of any tools that the risk and needs assessment system uses; and

(E) an evaluation of the rates

of recidivism among similarly classified prisoners to identify any unwarranted disparities, including disparities among similarly classified prisoners of different demographic groups, in such rates;

(5) make any revisions or updates to the risk and needs assessment system that the Attorney General determines appropriate pursuant to the review under paragraph (4), including updates to ensure that any disparities identified in paragraph (4)(E) are reduced to the greatest extent possible; and

(6) report to Congress in accordance with section 3634.

§ 3632. Development of risk and needs assessment system

(a) In general.-Not later than 210 days after the date of enactment of this subchapter, the Attorney General, in consultation with the Independent Review Committee authorized by the First Step Act of 2018, shall develop and release publicly on the Department of Justice website a risk and needs assessment system (referred to in this subchapter as the 'System'), which shall be used to-

(1) determine the recidivism risk of each prisoner as part of the intake process, and classify each prisoner as having minimum, low, medium, or high risk for recidivism;

(2) assess and determine, to the extent practicable, the risk of violent or serious misconduct of each prisoner;

(3) determine the type and amount of evidence-based recidivism reduction programming that is appropriate for each prisoner and assign each prisoner to such programming accordingly, and based on the prisoner's specific criminogenic needs, and in accordance with subsection (b);

(4) reassess the recidivism risk of each prisoner periodically, based on factors including indicators of progress, and of regression, that are dynamic and that can reasonably be expected to change while in

prison;

(5) reassign the prisoner to appropriate evidence-based recidivism reduction programs or productive activities based on the revised determination to ensure that-

(A) all prisoners at each risk level have a meaningful opportunity to reduce their classification during the period of incarceration;

(B) to address the specific criminogenic needs of the prisoner; and

(C) all prisoners are able to successfully participate in such programs;

(6) determine when to provide incentives and rewards for successful participation in evidence-based recidivism reduction programs or productive activities in accordance with subsection (e);

(7) determine when a prisoner is ready to transfer into prerelease custody or

super- vised release in accordance with section 3624; and

(8) determine the appropriate use of audio technology for program course materials with an understanding of dyslexia.

In carrying out this subsection, the Attorney General may use existing risk and needs assessment tools, as appropriate.

(b) Assignment of evidence-based recidivism reduction programs.-The System shall provide guidance on the type, amount, and intensity of evidence-based recidivism reduction programming and productive activities that shall be assigned for each prisoner, including-

(1) programs in which the Bureau of Prisons shall assign the prisoner to participate, according to the prisoner's specific criminogenic needs; and

(2) information on the best ways that the Bureau of Prisons can tailor the programs to the specific criminogenic needs of

each prisoner so as to most effectively lower each prisoner's risk of recidivism.

(c) Housing and assignment decisions.-The System shall provide guidance on program grouping and housing assignment determinations and, after accounting for the safety of each prisoner and other individuals at the prison, provide that prisoners with a similar risk level be grouped together in housing and assignment decisions to the extent practicable.

(d) Evidence-Based recidivism reduction program incentives and productive activities rewards.-The System shall provide incentives and rewards for prisoners to participate in and complete evidence-based recidivism reduction programs as follows:

(1) PHONE AND VISITATION PRIVILEGES.-A prisoner who is successfully participating in an evidence-based recidivism reduction program shall receive-

(A) phone privileges, or, if available, video conferencing privileges, for up to 30 minutes per day, and up to 510 minutes per month; and

(B) additional time for visitation at the prison, as determined by the warden of the prison.

(2) TRANSFER TO INSTITUTION CLOSER TO RELEASE RESIDENCE.-A prisoner who is successfully participating in an evidence-based recidivism reduction program shall be considered by the Bureau of Prisons for placement in a facility closer to the prisoner's release residence upon request from the prisoner and subject to-

(A) bed availability at the transfer facility;

(B) the prisoner's security designation; and

(C) the recommendation from the warden of the prison at which the prisoner is incarcerated at the time of making the request.

(3) ADDITIONAL POLICIES.-The Director of the Bureau of Prisons shall develop additional policies to provide appropriate incentives for successful participation and completion of evidence-based recidivism reduction programming. The incentives shall include not less than 2 of the following:

(A) Increased commissary spending limits and product offerings.

(B) Extended opportunities to access the email system.

(C) Consideration of transfer to preferred housing units (including transfer to different prison facilities).

(D) Other incentives solicited from prisoners and determined appropriate by the Director.

(4) TIME CREDITS.-

(A) IN GENERAL.-A prisoner, except for an ineligible prisoner under subparagraph (D), who successfully completes evidence-based recidivism reduction programming or productive activities, shall earn time credits as follows:

>(i) A prisoner shall earn 10 days of time credits for every 30 days of successful participation in evidence-based recidivism reduction programming or productive activities.

>(ii) A prisoner determined by the Bureau of Prisons to be at a minimum or low risk for recidivating, who, over 2 consecutive

assessments, has not increased their risk of recidivism, shall earn an additional 5 days of time credits for every 30 days of successful participation in evidence-based recidivism reduction programming or productive activities.

(B) AVAILABILITY.-A prisoner may not earn time credits under this paragraph for an evidence-based recidivism reduction program that the prisoner successfully completed-

(i) prior to the date of enactment of this subchapter; or

(ii) during official detention prior to the date that the prisoner's sentence commences under section 3585(a).

(C) APPLICATION OF TIME CREDITS TOWARD PRERELEASE CUSTODY OR SUPERVISED RELEASE.-Time credits earned under this paragraph by prisoners who success- fully participate in recidivism reduction programs or productive activities shall be applied toward time in prerelease custody or supervised release. The Director of the Bureau of Prisons shall transfer eligible prisoners, as determined under section 3624(g), into prerelease custody or supervised release.

(D) INELIGIBLE PRISONERS.-A prisoner is ineligible to receive time credits under this paragraph if the prisoner is serving a sentence for a conviction under any of the following provisions of law:

(i) Section 32, relating to destruction of aircraft or aircraft facilities.

(ii) Section 33, relating to destruction of motor vehicles or motor vehicle facilities.

(iii) Section 36, relating to drive-by shootings.

(iv) Section 81, relating to arson within special maritime and territorial jurisdiction.

(v) Section 111(b), relating to assaulting, resisting, or impeding certain officers or employees using a deadly or dangerous weapon or inflicting bodily injury.

(vi) Paragraph (1), (7), or (8) of section

113(a), relating to assault with intent to commit murder, assault resulting in substantial bodily injury to a spouse or intimate partner, a dating partner, or an individual who has not attained the age of 16 years, or assault of a spouse, intimate partner, or dating partner by strangling, suffocating, or attempting to strangle or suffocate.

(vii) Section 115, relating to influencing, impeding, or retaliating against a Federal official by injuring a family member, except for a threat made in violation of that section.

(viii) Section 116, relating to female genital mutilation.

(ix) Section 117, relating to domestic assault by a habitual offender.

(x) Any section of chapter 10, relating to biological weapons.

(xi) Any section of chapter 11B, relating to chemical weapons.

(xii) Section 351, relating to Congressional, Cabinet, and Supreme Court assassination, kidnapping, and assault.

(xiii) Section 521, relating to criminal street gangs.

(xiv) Section 751, relating to prisoners in custody of an institution or officer.

(xv) Section 793, relating to gathering, transmitting, or losing defense information.

(xvi) Section 794, relating to gathering or delivering defense information to aid a foreign government.

(xvii) Any section of chapter 39, relating to explosives and other dangerous articles, except for section 836 (relating to the transportation of fireworks into a State prohibiting sale or use).

(xviii) Section 842(p), relating to distribution of information relating to explosives, destructive devices, and weapons of mass destruction, but only if the conviction involved a weapon of mass destruction (as defined in section 2332a(c)).

(xix) Subsection (f)(3), (h), or (i) of section 844, relating to the use of fire or an explosive.

(xx) Section 871,

relating to threats against the President and successors to the Presidency.

(xxi) Section 879, relating to threats against former Presidents and certain other per- sons.

(xxii) Section 924(c), relating to unlawful possession or use of a firearm during and in relation to any crime of violence or drug trafficking crime.

(xxiii) Section 1030(a)(1), relating to fraud and related activity in connection with computers.

(xxiv) Section 1091,

relating to genocide.

(xxv) Any section of chapter 51, relating to homicide, except for section 1112 (relating to manslaughter), 1113 (relating to attempt to commit murder or manslaughter, but only if the conviction was for an attempt to commit manslaughter), 1115 (relating to misconduct or neglect of ship officers), or 1122 (relating to protection against the human immunodeficiency virus).

(xxvi) Any section of chapter 55, relating to kidnapping.

(xxvii) Any offense under chapter 77, relating to peonage, slavery, and trafficking in persons, except for sections 1593 through 1596.

(xxviii) Section 1751, relating to Presidential and Presidential staff assassination, kidnapping, and assault.

(xxix) Section 1791, relating to providing or possessing contraband in prison.

(xxx) Section 1792, relating to mutiny and riots.

(xxxi) Section 1841(a)(2)(C), relating to intentionally killing or attempting to kill an unborn child.

(xxxii) Section 1992, relating to terrorist attacks and other violence against railroad carriers and against mass transportation systems on land, on water, or through the air.

(xxxiii) Section 2113(e), relating to bank robbery resulting in death.

(xxxiv) Section 2118(c), relating to robberies and burglaries involving controlled sub- stances resulting in assault, putting in jeopardy the life of any person by the use of a dangerous weapon or device, or death.

(xxxv) Section 2119, relating to taking a motor vehicle (commonly referred to as 'car jacking').

(xxxvi) Any section of chapter 105, relating to sabotage, except for section 2152.

(xxxvii) Any section of chapter 109A, relating to sexual abuse.

(xxxviii) Section 2250, relating to failure to register as a sex offender.

(xxxix) Section 2251, relating to the sexual

exploitation of children.

(xl) Section 2251A, relating to the selling or buying of children.

(xli) Section 2252, relating to certain activities relating to material involving the sexual exploitation of minors.

(lii) Section 57(b) of the Atomic Energy Act of 1954 **(42 U.S.C. 2077(b))**, relating to the engagement or participation in the development or production of special nuclear material.

(liii) Section 92 of the Atomic Energy Act of

1954 **(42 U.S.C. 2122)**, relating to prohibitions governing atomic weapons.

(liv) Section 101 of the Atomic Energy Act of 1954 **(42 U.S.C. 2131)**, relating to the atomic energy license requirement.

(lv) Section 224 or 225 of the Atomic Energy Act of 1954 **(42 U.S.C. 2274, 2275)**, relating to the communication or receipt of restricted data.

(lvi) Section 236 of the Atomic Energy Act of 1954 **(42 U.S.C. 2284)**, relating to the sabotage of nuclear facilities or fuel.

(lvii) Section 60123(b) of title 49, relating to damaging or destroying a pipeline facility, but only if the conduct which led to the conviction involved a substantial risk of death or serious bodily injury.

(lviii) Section 401(a) of the Controlled Substances Act **(21 U.S.C. 841)**, relating to manufacturing or distributing a controlled substance in the case of a conviction for an offense described in subparagraph (A), (B), or (C) of subsection (b)(1) of that section for which death or serious bodily injury resulted from the use of such substance.

(lix) Section 276(a) of the Immigration and Nationality Act **(8 U.S.C. 1326)**, relating to the reentry of a removed alien, but only if the alien is described in paragraph (1) or (2) of subsection (b) of that section.

(lx) Section 277 of the Immigration and Nationality Act **(8 U.S.C. 1327)**, relating to aiding or assisting certain aliens to enter the United States.

(lxi) Section 278 of the Immigration and Nationality Act **(8 U.S.C. 1328)**, relating to the importation of an alien into the United States for an immoral purpose.

(lxii) Any section of the Export Administration Act of 1979 **(50 U.S.C. 4611 et seq.)**

(lxiii) Section 206 of the International Emergency Economic Powers Act **(50 U.S.C. 1705)**.

(lxiv) Section 601 of the National Security Act of 1947 **(50 U.S.C. 3121)**, relating to the protection of identities of certain United States undercover intelligence officers, agents, informants, and sources.

(lxv) Subparagraph (A)(i) or (B)(i) of section 401(b)(1) of the Controlled Substances Act **(21 U.S.C. 841(b)(1))** or paragraph (1)(A) or (2)(A) of section 1010(b) of the Controlled Substances Import and Export Act **(21 U.S.C. 960(b))**, relating to manufacturing, distributing, dispensing, or possessing with intent to manufacture, distribute, dispense, or knowingly importing or exporting, a mixture or substance containing a detectable amount of heroin if the sentencing court finds that the offender was an organizer, leader, manager, or supervisor of others in the offense, as determined under the guide- lines promulgated by the United States Sentencing Commission.

(lxvi) Subparagraph (A)(vi) or (B)(vi) of section 401(b)(1) of the Controlled Substances Act **(21 U.S.C. 841(b)(1))** or paragraph (1)(F) or (2)(F) of section 1010(b) of the Controlled Substances Import and Export Act **(21 U.S.C. 960(b))**, relating to manufacturing, distributing, dispensing, or possessing with intent to manufacture, distribute, or dispense, a mixture or substance containing a detectable amount of N-phenyl-N-[1-(2-phenylethyl)-4-piperidinyl] propanamide, or any analogue thereof.

(lxvii) Subparagraph (A)(viii) or (B)(viii) of section 401(b)(1) of the Controlled Substances Act **(21 U.S.C. 841(b)(1))** or paragraph (1)(H) or (2)(H) of section 1010(b) the Controlled Substances Import and Export Act **(21 U.S.C. 960(b))**, relating to manufacturing, distributing, dispensing, or possessing with intent to manufacture, distribute, or dispense, or knowingly importing or exporting, a mixture of substance containing a detectable amount of methamphetamine, its salts, isomers, or salts of its isomers, if the sentencing court finds that the offender was an organizer, leader, manager, or supervisor of others in the offense, as determined under the guidelines promulgated by the United States Sentencing Commission.

(lxviii) Subparagraph

(A) or (B) of section 401(b)(1) of the Controlled Substances Act **(21 U.S.C. 841(b)(1))** or paragraph (1) or (2) of section 1010(b) of the Controlled Substances Import and Export Act **(21 U.S.C. 960(b))**, relating to manufacturing, distributing, dispensing, or possessing with intent to manufacture, distribute, or dispense, a controlled substance, or knowingly importing or exporting a controlled substance, if the sentencing court finds that-

(I) the offense involved a

mixture or substance containing a detectable amount of N-phenyl-N-[1-(2-phenylethyl)-4-piperidinyl] propanamide, or any analogue thereof; and

(II) the offender was an organizer, leader, manager, or supervisor of others in the offense, as determined under the guidelines promulgated by the United States Sentencing

Commission.

(E) DEPORTABLE PRISONERS INELIGIBLE TO APPLY TIME CREDITS.-

(i) IN GENERAL.-A prisoner is ineligible to apply time credits under subparagraph (C) if the prisoner is the subject of a final order of removal under any provision of the immigration laws (as such term is defined in section 101(a)(17) of the Immigration and Nationality Act **(8 U.S.C. 1101(a)(17)))**.

(ii) PROCEEDINGS. -The Attorney General, in consultation with the Secretary of Homeland Security, shall ensure that any alien described in section 212 or 237 of the Immigration and Nationality Act **(8 U.S.C. 1182, 1227)** who seeks to earn time credits are subject to proceedings described in section 238(a) of that Act **(8 U.S.C. 1228(a))** at a date as early as practicable during the prisoner's incarceration.

(5) RISK REASSESSMENTS AND LEVEL ADJUSTMENT.-A prisoner who successfully participates in evidence-based recidivism reduction programming or productive activities shall receive periodic risk reassessments not less often than annually, and a prisoner determined to be at a medium or high risk of recidivating and who has less than 5 years until his or her projected release date shall receive more frequent risk reassessments. If the

reassessment shows that the prisoner's risk of recidivating or specific needs have changed, the Bureau of Prisons shall update the determination of the prison- er's risk of recidivating or information regarding the prisoner's specific needs and reassign the prisoner to appropriate evidence-based recidivism reduction programming or productive activities based on such changes.

(6) RELATION TO OTHER INCENTIVE PROGRAMS.-The incentives described in this subsection shall be in addition to any other rewards or incentives for which a prisoner may be eligible.

(e) Penalties.-The Director of the Bureau of Prisons shall develop guidelines for the reduction of rewards and incentives earned under subsection (d) for prisoners who violate prison rules or evidence-based recidivism reduction program or productive activity rules, which shall provide-

(1) general levels of violations and resulting reductions;

(2) that any reduction that includes the loss of time credits shall require written notice to the prisoner, shall be limited to time credits that a prisoner earned as of the date of the prisoner's rule violation, and shall not include any future time credits that the prisoner may earn; and

(3) for a procedure to restore time credits that a prisoner lost as a result of a rule violation, based on the prisoner's individual progress after the date of the rule violation.

(f) Bureau of Prisons training.-The Attorney General shall develop and implement training programs for Bureau of Prisons officers and employees responsible for administering the System, which shall include-

(1) initial training to educate officers and employees on how to use the System in an appropriate and consistent manner, as well as the reasons for using the System;

(2) continuing education;

(3) periodic training updates; and

(4) a requirement that such officers and employees demonstrate competence in administering the System, including interrater reliability, on a biannual basis.

(g) Quality assurance.-In order to ensure that the Bureau of Prisons is using the System in an appropriate and consistent manner, the Attorney General shall monitor and assess the use of the System, which shall include conducting annual audits of the Bureau of Prisons regarding the use of the System.

(h) Dyslexia screening.-

(1) SCREENING.-The Attorney General shall incorporate a dyslexia screening program into the System, including by screening for dyslexia during-

(A) the intake process; and

(B) each periodic risk reassessment of a prisoner.

(2) TREATMENT.-The Attorney General shall incorporate programs designed to treat dyslexia into the evidence-based recidivism reduction programs or productive activities required to be implemented under this section. The Attorney General may also incorporate programs designed to treat other learning disabilities.

§ 3633. Evidence-based recidivism reduction program and recommendations

(a) In general.-Prior to releasing the System, in consultation with the Independent Review Committee authorized by the First Step Act of 2018, the Attorney General shall-

(1) review the effectiveness of evidence-based recidivism reduction programs that exist as of the date of enactment of this subchapter in prisons operated by the Bureau of Pris- ons;

(2) review available information

regarding the effectiveness of evidence-based recidivism reduction programs and productive activities that exist in State-operated prisons throughout the United States;

(3) identify the most effective evidence-based recidivism reduction programs;

(4) review the policies for entering into evidence-based recidivism reduction partner- ships described in section 3621(h)(5); and

(5) direct the Bureau of Prisons regarding-

(A) evidence-based recidivism reduction programs;

(B) the ability for faith-based organizations to function as a provider of educational evidence-based programs outside of the religious classes and services provided through the Chaplaincy; and

(C) the addition of any new

effective evidence-based recidivism reduction programs that the Attorney General finds.

(b) Review and recommendations regarding dyslexia mitigation.-In carrying out sub- section (a), the Attorney General shall consider the prevalence and mitigation of dyslexia in prisons, including by-

(1) reviewing statistics on the prevalence of dyslexia, and the effectiveness of any pro- grams implemented to mitigate the effects of dyslexia, in prisons operated by the Bureau of Prisons and State-operated prisons throughout the United States; and

(2) incorporating the findings of the Attorney General under paragraph (1) of this sub- section into any directives given to the Bureau of Prisons under paragraph (5) of subsection (a).

§ 3634. Report

Beginning on the date that is 2 years after the date of enactment of this subchapter, and annually thereafter for a period of 5 years, the Attorney General shall submit a report to the Committees on the Judiciary of the Senate and the House of Representatives and the Subcommittees on Commerce, Justice, Science, and Related Agencies of the Committees on Appropriations of the Senate and the House of Representatives that contains the following:

(1) A summary of the activities and accomplishments of the Attorney General in carrying out this Act.

(2) A summary and assessment of the types and effectiveness of the evidence-based recidivism reduction programs and productive activities in prisons operated by the Bureau of Prisons, including-

(A) evidence about which programs have been shown to reduce recidivism;

(B) the capacity of each program and activity at each prison, including the number of prisoners along with the recidivism risk of each prisoner enrolled in each program; and

(C) identification of any gaps or shortages in capacity of such programs and activities.

(3) Rates of recidivism among individuals who have been released from Federal prison, based on the following criteria:

(A) The primary offense of conviction.

(B) The length of the sentence imposed and served.

(C) The Bureau of Prisons facility or facilities in which the prisoner's sentence was served.

(D) The evidence-based recidivism reduction programming that the prisoner success- fully completed, if any.

(E) The prisoner's assessed and reassessed risk of recidivism.

(F) The productive activities that the prisoner successfully completed, if any.

(4) The status of prison work programs at facilities operated by the Bureau of Prisons, including-

(A) a strategy to expand the availability of such programs without reducing job opportunities for workers in the United States who are not in the custody of the Bureau of Prisons, including the feasibility of prisoners manufacturing products purchased by Federal agencies that are manufactured overseas;

(B) an assessment of the feasibility of expanding such programs, consistent with the strategy required under subparagraph (A), with the goal that 5 years after the date of enactment of this subchapter, not less than 75 percent of eligible minimum- and low-risk offenders have the opportunity to participate in a prison work program for not less than 20 hours per week; and

(C) a detailed discussion of

legal authorities that would be useful or necessary to achieve the goals described in subparagraphs (A) and (B).

(5) An assessment of the Bureau of Prisons' compliance with section 3621(h).

(6) An assessment of progress made toward carrying out the purposes of this subchapter, including any savings associated with-

(A) the transfer of prisoners into prerelease custody or supervised release under section 3624(g), including savings resulting from the avoidance or deferral of future construction, acquisition, and operations costs; and

(B) any decrease in recidivism that may be attributed to the System or the increase in evidence-based recidivism reduction programs required under this subchapter.

(7) An assessment of budgetary

savings resulting from this subchapter, including-

(A) a summary of the amount of savings resulting from the transfer of prisoners into prerelease custody under this chapter, including savings resulting from the avoidance or deferral of future construction, acquisition, or operations costs;

(B) a summary of the amount of savings resulting from any decrease in recidivism that may be attributed to the implementation of the risk and needs assessment system or the increase in recidivism reduction programs and productive activities required by this subchapter;

(C) a strategy to reinvest the savings described in subparagraphs (A) and (B) in other-

(i) Federal, State, and local law enforcement activities; and

(ii) expansions of recidivism reduction programs and productive activities in the Bureau of Prisons; and

(D) a description of how the reduced expenditures on Federal corrections and the budgetary savings resulting from this subchapter are currently being used and will be used to-

(i) increase investment in law enforcement and crime prevention to combat gangs of national significance and high-level drug traffickers through the High Intensity Drug Trafficking Areas Program and other task forces;

(ii) hire, train, and

equip law enforcement officers and prosecutors; and

(iii) promote crime reduction programs using evidence based practices and strategic planning to help reduce crime and criminal recidivism.

(8) Statistics on—

(A) the prevalence of dyslexia among prisoners in prisons operated by the Bureau of Prisons; and

(B) any change in the effectiveness of dyslexia mitigation programs among such prisoners that may be attributed to the incorporation of dyslexia screening into the System and of dyslexia treatment into the evidence-based recidivism reduction programs, as required under this chapter.

§ 3635. Definitions

In this subchapter the following definitions apply:

(1) DYSLEXIA.-The term 'dyslexia' means an unexpected difficulty in reading for an individual who has the intelligence to be a much better reader, most commonly caused by a difficulty in the phonological processing (the appreciation of the individual sounds of spoken language), which affects the ability of an individual to speak, read, and spell.

(2) DYSLEXIA SCREENING PROGRAM.-The term 'dyslexia screening program' means a screening program for dyslexia that is-

(A) evidence based (as defined in section 8101(21) of the Elementary and Secondary Education Act of 1965 (20 U.S.C. 7801(21))) with proven psychometrics for validity;

(B) efficient and low-cost; and

(C) readily available.

(3) EVIDENCE-BASED RECIDIVISM REDUCTION PROGRAM.-The term 'evidence-based recidivism reduction program' means either a group or individual activity that-

(A) has been shown by empirical evidence to reduce recidivism or is based on research indicating that it is likely to be effective in reducing recidivism;

(B) is designed to help prisoners succeed in their communities upon release from prison; and

(C) may include-

(i) social learning and communication, interpersonal, anti bullying, rejection response, and other life skills;

(ii) family relationship building, structured parent-child interaction, and parenting skills;

(iii) classes on morals or ethics;

(iv) academic classes;

(v) cognitive behavioral treatment;

(vi) mentoring;

(vii) substance abuse treatment;

(viii) vocational training;

(ix) faith-based classes

or services;

(x) civic engagement and reintegrative community services;

(xi) a prison job, including through a prison work program;

(xii) victim impact classes or other restorative justice programs; and

(xiii) trauma counseling and trauma-informed support programs.

(4) PRISONER.-The term 'prisoner' means a person who has been sentenced to a term of imprisonment pursuant to a conviction for a Federal criminal offense, or a person in the custody of the Bureau of Prisons.

(5) PRODUCTIVE ACTIVITY.-The term 'productive activity' means either a group or individual activity that is designed to allow prisoners determined as having a minimum or low risk of recidivating to remain productive and thereby maintain a minimum or low risk of recidivating, and may include the delivery of the programs described in paragraph (1)[1] to other prisoners.

(6) RISK AND NEEDS ASSESSMENT TOOL.- The term 'risk and needs assessment tool' means an objective and statistically validated method through which information is collected and evaluated to determine-

(A) as part of the intake process, the risk that a prisoner will recidivate upon release from prison;

(B) the recidivism reduction

---

[1] But See 18 U.S.Code 3635 (2019), n. 1., Probably should be paragraph (3). *Id.*

programs that will best minimize the risk that the prisoner will recidivate upon release from prison; and

(C) the periodic reassessment of risk that a prisoner will recidivate upon release from prison, based on factors including indicators of progress and of regression, that are dynamic and that can reasonably be expected to change while in prison..

(b) Clerical amendment.-The table of subchapters for chapter 229 of title 18, United States Code, is amended by adding at the end the following:

"D. Risk and Needs Assessment 3631."

SEC. 102. Implementation of system and recommendations by Bureau of Prisons.

(a) Implementation of system generally.- **Section 3621 of title 18**, United States Code, is amended by adding at the end the following:

"(h) Implementation of risk and needs assessment system.-

(1) IN GENERAL.-Not later than 180 days after the Attorney General completes and releases the risk and needs assessment system (referred to in this subsection as the 'System') developed under subchapter D, the Director of the Bureau of Prisons shall, in accordance with that subchapter-

(A) implement and complete the initial intake risk and needs assessment for each prisoner (including for each prisoner who was a prisoner prior to the effective date of this subsection), regardless of the prisoner's length of imposed term of imprisonment, and begin to assign prisoners to appropriate evidence-based recidivism reduction programs based on that determination;

(B) begin to expand the

effective evidence-based recidivism reduction programs and productive activities it offers and add any new evidence based recidivism reduction programs and productive activities necessary to effectively implement the System; and

(C) begin to implement the other risk and needs assessment tools necessary to effectively implement the System over time, while prisoners are participating in and completing the effective evidence-based recidivism reduction programs and productive activities.

(2) PHASE-IN.-In order to carry out paragraph (1), so that every prisoner has the opportunity to participate in and complete the type and amount of evidence-based recidivism reduction programs or productive activities they need, and be reassessed for recidivism risk as necessary to effectively implement the System, the Bureau of Prisons shall-

(A) provide such evidence-based recidivism reduction

programs and productive activities for all prisoners before the date that is 2 years after the date on which the Bureau of Prisons completes a risk and needs assessment for each prisoner under paragraph (1) (A); and

(B) develop and validate the risk and needs assessment tool to be used in the reassessments of risk of recidivism, while prisoners are participating in and completing evidence-based recidivism reduction programs and productive activities.

(3) PRIORITY DURING PHASE-IN.-During the 2-year period described in paragraph (2) (A), the priority for such programs and activities shall be accorded based on a prisoner's proximity to release date.

(4) PRELIMINARY EXPANSION OF EVIDENCE-BASED RECIDIVISM REDUCTION PROGRAMS AND AUTHORITY TO USE INCENTIVES.-Beginning on the date of enactment of this subsection, the Bureau of Prisons may begin to expand any

evidence-based recidivism reduction programs and productive activities that exist at a prison as of such date, and may offer to prisoners who successfully participate in such programs and activities the incentives and rewards described in subchapter D.

(5) RECIDIVISM REDUCTION PARTNERSHIPS.- In order to expand evidence-based recidivism reduction programs and productive activities, the Attorney General shall develop policies for the warden of each prison of the Bureau of Prisons to enter into partnerships, subject to the availability of appropriations, with any of the following:

(A) Nonprofit and other private organizations, including faith-based, art, and community-based organizations that will deliver recidivism reduction programming on a paid or volunteer basis.

(B) Institutions of higher education (as defined in section 101 of the Higher Education Act of 1965 **(20 U.S.C. 1001))** that will deliver instruction on a paid or volunteer basis.

> (C) Private entities that will-
>
>> (i) deliver vocational training and certifications;
>>
>> (ii) provide equipment to facilitate vocational training or employment opportunities for prisoners;
>>
>> (iii) employ prisoners; or
>>
>> (iv) assist prisoners in prerelease custody or supervised release in finding employment.
>
> (D) Industry-sponsored organizations that will deliver workforce development and training, on a paid or volunteer

basis.

(6) REQUIREMENT TO PROVIDE PROGRAMS TO ALL PRISONERS; PRIORITY.-The Director of the Bureau of Prisons shall provide all prisoners with the opportunity to actively participate in evidence-based recidivism reduction programs or productive activities, according to their specific criminogenic needs, throughout their entire term of incarceration. Priority for participation in recidivism reduction programs shall be given to medium-risk and high-risk prisoners, with access to productive activities given to minimum-risk and low-risk prisoners.

(7) DEFINITIONS.-The terms in this subsection have the meaning given those terms in section 3635."

(b) Prerelease custody.-

(1) IN GENERAL.-**Section 3624 of title 18**, United States Code, is amended-

(A) in subsection (b)(1)-

(i) by striking , beyond the time served, of up to 54 days at the end of each year of the prisoner's term of imprisonment, beginning at the end of the first year of the term, and inserting of up to 54 days for each year of the prisoner's sentence imposed by the court,; and

(ii) by striking credit for the last year or portion of a year of the term of imprisonment shall be prorated and credited within the last six weeks of the sentence and inserting credit for the last year of a term of imprisonment shall be credited on the first day of the last year of the term of imprisonment; and

(B) by adding at the end the following:

"(g) Prerelease custody or supervised release for risk and needs assessment system participants.-

(1) ELIGIBLE PRISONERS.-This subsection applies in the case of a prisoner (as such term is defined in section 3635) who-

(A) has earned time credits under the risk and needs assessment system developed under subchapter D (referred to in this subsection as the 'System') in an amount that is equal to the remainder of the prisoner's imposed term of imprisonment;

(B) has shown through the periodic risk reassessments a demonstrated recidivism risk reduction or has maintained a minimum or low recidivism risk, during the prisoner's term of imprisonment;

(C) has had the remainder of the prisoner's imposed term of imprisonment computed under applicable law; and

(D)
(i) in the case of a prisoner being placed in prerelease custody, the prisoner-

(I) has been determined under the System to be a minimum or low risk to recidivate pursuant to the last 2 reassessments of the prisoner; or

(II) has had a

petition to be transferred to prerelease custody or supervised release approved by the warden of the prison, after the warden's determination that-

(aa) the prisoner would not be a danger to society if transferred to prerelease custody or supervised release;

(bb) the

prisoner has made a good faith effort to lower their recidivism risk through participation in recidivism reduction programs or productive activities; and

(cc) the prisoner is unlikely to recidivate;

or

(ii) in the case of a prisoner being placed in supervised release, the prisoner has been determined under the System to be a minimum or low risk to recidivate pursuant to the last reassessment of the prisoner.

(2) TYPES OF PRERELEASE CUSTODY.-A prisoner shall be placed in prerelease custody as follows:

(A) HOME CONFINEMENT.-

(i) IN GENERAL.-A prisoner placed in prerelease custody pursuant to this subsection who is placed in home confinement shall-

>(I) be subject to 24-hour electronic monitoring that enables the prompt identification of the prisoner, location, and time, in the case of any violation of subclause (II);

>(II) remain in the prisoner's residence, except that the prisoner may leave the prisoner's home in order to, subject to the approval of the

Director of the Bureau of Prisons-

(aa) perform a job or job related activities, including an apprenticeship, or participate in job seeking activities;

(bb) participate in evidence based recidivism reduction programming or productive activities assigned by the System, or similar activities;

(cc) perform community service;

(dd) participate in crime victim restoration activities;

(ee) receive

medical treatment;

(ff) attend religious activities; or

(gg) participate in other family related activities that facilitate the prisoner's successful reentry such as a family funeral, a family wedding, or to visit a family member who is seriously ill; and

(III) comply with such other conditions as the Director determines appropriate.

(ii) ALTERNATE MEANS OF MONITORING.-If the electronic monitoring of a prisoner described in clause (i)(I) is infeasible for technical or religious reasons, the Director of the Bureau of Prisons may use alternative means of monitoring a prisoner placed in home confinement that the Director determines are as effective or more effective than the electronic monitoring described in clause (i)(I).

(iii) MODIF-ICATIONS.-The Director of the Bureau of Prisons may modify the conditions described in clause (i) if the Director determines that a compelling reason exists to do so, and that the prisoner has demonstrated exemplary compliance with such conditions.

(iv) DURATION.- Except as provided in

paragraph (4), a prisoner who is placed in home confinement shall remain in home confinement until the prisoner has served not less than 85 percent of the prisoner's imposed term of imprisonment.

(B) RESIDENTIAL REENTRY CENTER.-A prisoner placed in prerelease custody pursuant to this subsection who is placed at a residential reentry center shall be subject to such conditions as the Director of the Bureau of Prisons determines appropriate.

(3) SUPERVISED RELEASE.-If the sentencing court included as a part of the prisoner's sentence a requirement that the prisoner be placed on a term of supervised release after imprisonment pursuant to section 3583, the Director of the Bureau of Prisons may transfer the prisoner to begin any such term of supervised release at an earlier date, not to exceed 12 months, based on the application of

time credits under section 3632.

(4) DETERMINATION OF CONDITIONS.-In determining appropriate conditions for prisoners placed in prerelease custody pursuant to this subsection, the Director of the Bureau of Prisons shall, to the extent practicable, provide that increasingly less restrictive conditions shall be imposed on prisoners who demonstrate continued compliance with the conditions of such prerelease custody, so as to most effectively prepare such prisoners for reentry.

(5) VIOLATIONS OF CONDITIONS.-If a prisoner violates a condition of the prisoner's prerelease custody, the Director of the Bureau of Prisons may impose such additional conditions on the prisoner's prerelease custody as the Director of the Bureau of Prisons determines appropriate, or revoke the prisoner's prerelease custody and require the prisoner to serve the remainder of the term of imprisonment to which the prisoner was sentenced, or any portion thereof, in prison. If the violation is nontechnical in nature, the Director of the

Bureau of Prisons shall revoke the prisoner's prerelease custody.

(6) ISSUANCE OF GUIDELINES.-The Attorney General, in consultation with the Assistant Director for the Office of Probation and Pretrial Services, shall issue guidelines for use by the Bureau of Prisons in determining-

(A) the appropriate type of prerelease custody or supervised release and level of supervision for a prisoner placed on prerelease custody pursuant to this subsection; and

(B) consequences for a violation of a condition of such prerelease custody by such a prisoner, including a return to prison and a reassessment of evidence-based recidivism risk level under the System.

(7) AGREEMENTS WITH UNITED STATES PROBATION AND PRETRIAL SERVICES.- The Director of the Bureau of Prisons shall, to the greatest extent

practicable, enter into agreements with United States Probation and Pretrial Services to supervise prisoners placed in home confinement under this subsection. Such agreements shall-

(A) authorize United States Probation and Pretrial Services to exercise the authority granted to the Director pursuant to paragraphs (3) and (4); and

(B) take into account the resource requirements of United States Probation and Pretrial Services as a result of the transfer of Bureau of Prisons prisoners to prerelease custody or supervised release.

(8) ASSISTANCE.-United States Probation and Pretrial Services shall, to the greatest extent practicable, offer assistance to any prisoner not under its supervision during pre release custody under this subsection.

(9) MENTORING, REENTRY, AND SPIRITUAL SERVICES.-Any prerelease custody into which a prisoner is placed under

this subsection may not include a condition prohibiting the prisoner from receiving mentoring, reentry, or spiritual services from a person who provided such services to the prisoner while the prisoner was incarcerated, except that the warden of the facility at which the prisoner was incarcerated may waive the requirement under this paragraph if the warden finds that the provision of such ser- vices would pose a significant security risk to the prisoner, persons who provide such services, or any other person. The warden shall provide written notice of any such waiver to the person providing such services and to the prisoner.

(10) TIME LIMITS INAPPLICABLE.- The time limits under subsections (b) and (c) shall not apply to prerelease custody under this subsection.

(11) PRERELEASE CUSTODY CAPACITY.-The Director of the Bureau of Prisons shall ensure there is sufficient prerelease custody capacity to accommodate all eligible prisoners..

(2) EFFECTIVE DATE.-The amendments made by this subsection shall take effect beginning on the date that the Attorney General completes and releases the risk and needs assessment system under subchapter D of chapter 229 of title 18, United States Code, as added by section 101(a) of this Act.

(3) APPLICABILITY.- The amendments made by this subsection shall apply with respect to offenses committed before, on, or after the date of enactment of this Act, except that such amendments shall not apply with respect to offenses committed before November 1, 1987.

SEC. 103. GAO Report

Not later than 2 years after the Director of the Bureau of Prisons implements the risk and needs assessment system under section 3621 of title 18, United States Code, and every 2 years thereafter, the Comptroller General of the United States shall conduct an audit of the use of the risk and needs assessment

system at Bureau of Prisons facilities. The audit shall include analysis of the following:

(1) Whether inmates are being assessed under the risk and needs assessment system with the frequency required under such section 3621 of title 18, United States Code.

(2) Whether the Bureau of Prisons is able to offer recidivism reduction programs and productive activities (as such terms are defined in section 3635 of title 18, United States Code, as added by section 101(a) of this Act).

(3) Whether the Bureau of Prisons is offering the type, amount, and intensity of recidivism reduction programs and productive activities for prisoners to earn the maximum amount of time credits for which they are eligible.

(4) Whether the Attorney General is carrying out the duties under section 3631(b) of title 18, United States Code, as added by section 101(a) of this Act.

(5) Whether officers and employees of the Bureau of Prisons are receiving the training described in section 3632(f) of title 18, United States Code, as added by section 101(a) of this Act.

(6) Whether the Bureau of Prisons offers work assignments to all prisoners who might benefit from such an assignment.

(7) Whether the Bureau of Prisons transfers prisoners to prerelease custody or super- vised release as soon as they are eligible for such a transfer under section 3624(g) of title 18, United States Code, as added by section 102(b) of this Act.

(8) The rates of recidivism among similarly classified prisoners to identify any unwarranted disparities, including disparities among similarly classified prisoners of different demographic groups, in such rates.

SEC. 104. Authorization of appropriations.

(a) In general.-There is authorized to be

appropriated to carry out this title $75,000,000 for each of fiscal years 2019 through 2023. Of the amount appropriated under this subsection, 80 percent shall be reserved for use by the Director of the Bureau of Prisons to implement the system under section 3621(h) of title 18, United States Code, as added by section 102(a) of this Act.

(b) Savings.-It is the sense of Congress that any savings associated with reductions in recidivism that result from this title should be reinvested-

(1) to supplement funding for programs that increase public safety by providing resources to State and local law enforcement officials, including for the adoption of innovative technologies and information sharing capabilities;

(2) into evidence-based recidivism reduction programs offered by the Bureau of Prisons; and

(3) into ensuring eligible prisoners

have access to such programs and productive activities offered by the Bureau of Prisons.

SEC. 105. Rules Of Construction.

Nothing in this Act, or the amendments made by this Act, may be construed to provide authority to place a prisoner in prerelease custody or supervised release who is serving a term of imprisonment pursuant to a conviction for an offense under the laws of one of the 50 States, or of a territory or possession of the United States or to amend or affect the enforcement of the immigration laws, as defined in section 101 of the Immigration and Nationality Act **(8 U.S.C. 1101).**

SEC. 106. Faith Based Considerations

(a) In general.- In considering any program, treatment, regimen, group, company, charity, person, or entity of any kind under any provision of this Act, or the amendments made by this Act, the fact that it may be or is faith-based may not be a basis for any discrimination against it in any manner or for any purpose.

(b) Eligibility for earned time credit.-Participation in a faith-based program, treatment, or regimen may qualify a prisoner for earned time credit under subchapter D of chapter 229 of title 18, United States Code, as added by section 101(a) of this Act, however, the Director of the Bureau of Prisons shall ensure that non-faith-based programs that qualify for earned time credit are offered at each Bureau of Prisons facility in addition to any such faith-based programs.

(c) Limitation on activities.-A group, company, charity, person, or entity may not engage in explicitly religious activities using direct financial assistance made available under this title or the amendments made by this title.

(d) Rule of construction.-Nothing in this Act, or the amendments made by this Act, may be construed to amend any requirement under Federal law or the Constitution of the United States regarding funding for faith-based programs or activities.

SEC. 107. Independent Review Committee.

(a) In general.-The Attorney General shall consult with an Independent Review Committee in carrying out the Attorney General's duties under sections 3631(b), 3632 and 3633 of title 18, United States Code, as added by section 101(a) of this Act.

(b) Formation of Independent Review Committee.-The National Institute of Justice shall select a nonpartisan and nonprofit organization with expertise in the study and development of risk and needs assessment tools to host the Independent Review Committee. The Independent Review Committee shall be established not later than 30 days after the date of enactment of this Act.

(c) Appointment of Independent Review Committee.-The organization selected by the National Institute of Justice shall appoint not fewer than 6 members to the Independent Review Committee.

(d) Composition of the Independent

Review Committee.-The members of the Independent Review Committee shall all have expertise in risk and needs assessment systems and shall include-

(1) 2 individuals who have published peer-reviewed scholarship about risk and needs assessments in both corrections and community settings;

(2) 2 corrections practitioners who have developed and implemented a risk assessment tool in a corrections system or in a community supervision setting, including 1 with prior experience working within the Bureau of Prisons; and

(3) 1 individual with expertise in assessing risk assessment implementation.

(e) Duties of the Independent Review Committee.-The Independent Review Committee shall assist the Attorney General in carrying out the Attorney General's duties under sections 3631(b), 3632 and 3633 of title 18, United States Code, as added by section 101 (a) of this Act, including by assisting in-

(1) conducting a review of the existing prisoner risk and needs assessment systems in operation on the date of enactment of this Act;

(2) developing recommendations regarding evidence-based recidivism reduction programs and productive activities;

(3) conducting research and data analysis on-

(A) evidence-based recidivism reduction programs relating to the use of prisoner risk and needs assessment tools;

(B) the most effective and efficient uses of such programs; and

(C) which evidence-based recidivism reduction programs are the most effective at reducing recidivism, and the type, amount, and intensity of programming that most effectively reduces the risk of recidivism; and

(4) reviewing and validating the risk and needs assessment system.

(f) Bureau of Prisons cooperation.-The Director of the Bureau of Prisons shall assist the Independent Review Committee in performing the Committee's duties and promptly respond to requests from the Committee for access to Bureau of Prisons facilities, personnel, and information.

(g) Report.-Not later than 2 years after the date of enactment of this Act, the Independent Review Committee shall submit to the Committee on the Judiciary and the Subcommittee on Commerce, Justice, Science, and Related Agencies of the Committee on Appropriations of the Senate and the Committee on the Judiciary and the Subcommittee on Commerce, Justice, Science, and Related Agencies of the Committee on Appropriations of the House of Representatives a report that includes-

(1) a list of all offenses of conviction for which prisoners were ineligible to

receive time credits under section 3632(d)(4)(D) of title 18, United States Code, as added by section 101(a) of this Act, and for each offense the number of prisoners excluded, including demographic percentages by age, race, and sex;

(2) the criminal history categories of prisoners ineligible to receive time credits under section 3632(d)(4)(D) of title 18, United States Code, as added by section 101(a) of this Act, and for each category the number of prisoners excluded, including demographic percentages by age, race, and sex;

(3) the number of prisoners ineligible to apply time credits under section 3632(d)(4)(D) of title 18, United States Code, as added by section 101(a) of this Act, who do not participate in recidivism reduction programming or productive activities, including the demographic percentages by age, race, and sex;

(4) any recommendations for modifications to section 3632(d)(4)(D) of title 18, United States Code, as added by section 101(a) of this Act, and any other

recommendations regarding recidivism reduction.

(h) Termination.-The Independent Review Committee shall terminate on the date that is 2 years after the date on which the risk and needs assessment system authorized by sections 3632 and 3633 of title 18, United States Code, as added by section 101(a) of this Act, is released.

TITLE II Bureau of Prisons secure firearms storage

SEC. 201. Short Title.

This title may be cited as the Lieutenant Osvaldo Albarati Correctional Officer Self-Protection Act of 2018.

SEC. 202. Secure Firearms Storage.

(a) In general.-Chapter 303 of title 18, United States Code, is amended by adding at the end the following:

§ 4050. Secure firearms storage

(a) Definitions.-In this section-

(1) the term 'employee' means a qualified law enforcement officer employed by the Bureau of Prisons; and

(2) the terms 'firearm' and 'qualified law enforcement officer' have the meanings given those terms under section 926B.

(b) Secure firearms storage.-The Director of the Bureau of Prisons shall ensure that each chief executive officer of a Federal penal or correctional institution-

(1)
(A) provides a secure storage area located outside of the secure perimeter of the institution for employees to store firearms; or

(B) allows employees to store firearms in a vehicle lockbox approved by the Director of the Bureau of Prisons; and

(2) notwithstanding any other provision of law, allows employees to carry concealed firearms on the premises outside of the secure perimeter of the institution..

(b) Technical and conforming amendment.-The table of sections for chapter 303 of title 18, United States Code, is amended by adding at the end the following:

"4050. Secure firearms storage."

TITLE III Restraints on pregnant prisoners prohibited

SEC. 301. Use of restraints on prisoners during the period of pregnancy and postpartum recovery prohibited.

(a) In general.-Chapter 317 of title 18, United States Code, is amended by inserting after section 4321 the following:

§ 4322. Use of restraints on prisoners during the period of pregnancy, labor, and postpartum recovery prohibited

(a) Prohibition.-Except as provided in subsection (b), beginning on the date on which pregnancy is confirmed by a healthcare professional, and ending at the conclusion of postpartum recovery, a prisoner in the custody of the Bureau of Prisons, or in the custody of the United States Marshals Service pursuant to section 4086, shall not be placed in restraints.

(b) Exceptions.-

(1) IN GENERAL.-The prohibition under subsection (a) shall not apply if-

(A) an appropriate corrections official, or a United States marshal, as applicable, makes a determination that the prisoner-

> (i) is an immediate and credible flight risk that cannot reasonably be prevented by other means; or

(ii) poses an immediate and serious threat of harm to herself or others that cannot reasonably be prevented by other means; or

(B) a healthcare professional responsible for the health and safety of the prisoner determines that the use of restraints is appropriate for the medical safety of the prisoner.

(2) LEAST RESTRICTIVE RESTRAINTS.-In the case that restraints are used pursuant to an exception under paragraph (1), only the least restrictive restraints necessary to pre- vent the harm or risk of escape described in paragraph (1) may be used.

(3) APPLICATION.-

(A) IN GENERAL.-The exceptions under paragraph (1) may not be applied-

(i) to place restraints around the ankles, legs, or waist of a prisoner;

(ii) to restrain a prisoner's hands behind her back;

(iii) to restrain a prisoner using 4-point restraints; or

(iv) to attach a prisoner to another prisoner.

(B) MEDICAL REQUEST.-Notwithstanding paragraph (1), upon the request of a healthcare professional who is responsible for the health and safety of a prisoner, a corrections official or United States marshal, as applicable, shall refrain from using restraints on the prisoner or shall remove restraints used on the prisoner.

(c) Reports.-

(1) REPORT TO THE DIRECTOR AND HEALTHCARE PROFESSIONAL.-If a corrections official or United States marshal uses restraints on a prisoner under subsection (b)(1), that official or marshal shall submit, not later than 30 days after placing the prisoner in restraints, to the Director of the Bureau of Prisons or the Director of the United States Marshals Service, as applicable, and to the healthcare professional responsible for the health and safety of the prisoner, a written report that describes the facts and circum- stances surrounding the use of restraints, and includes-

(A) the reasoning upon which the determination to use restraints was made;

(B) the details of the use of restraints, including the type of restraints used and length of time during which restraints were used; and

(C) any resulting physical effects on the prisoner observed by or known to the corrections official or United States marshal, as applicable.

(2) SUPPLEMENTAL REPORT TO THE DIRECTOR.-Upon receipt of a report under para- graph (1), the healthcare professional responsible for the health and safety of the prisoner may submit to the Director such information as the healthcare professional determines is relevant to the use of restraints on the prisoner.

(3) REPORT TO JUDICIARY COMMITTEES.-

(A) IN GENERAL.-Not later than 1 year after the date of enactment of this section, and annually thereafter, the Director of the Bureau of Prisons and the Director of the United States Marshals Service shall each submit to the Judiciary Committee of the Senate and of the House of Representatives a report that certifies compliance with this section and includes the information required to be reported under paragraph (1).

(B) PERSONALLY IDENTIFIABLE INFORMATION.-The report under this paragraph shall not contain any personally identifiable information of any prisoner.

(d) Notice.-Not later than 48 hours after the confirmation of a prisoner's pregnancy by a healthcare professional, that prisoner shall be notified by an appropriate healthcare professional, corrections official, or United States marshal, as applicable, of the restrictions on the use of restraints under this section.

(e) Violation reporting process.-The Director of the Bureau of Prisons, in consultation with the Director of the United States Marshals Service, shall establish a process through which a prisoner may report a violation of this section.

(f) Training.-

(1) IN GENERAL.-The Director of the Bureau of Prisons and the Director of the United States Marshals Service shall each develop training guidelines regarding the use of restraints on female prisoners during the period of pregnancy, labor, and postpartum recovery,

and shall incorporate such guidelines into appropriate training programs. Such training guidelines shall include-

(A) how to identify certain symptoms of pregnancy that require immediate referral to a healthcare professional;

(B) circumstances under which the exceptions under subsection (b) would apply;

(C) in the case that an exception under subsection (b) applies, how to apply restraints in a way that does not harm the prisoner, the fetus, or the neonate;

(D) the information required to be reported under subsection (c); and

(E) the right of a healthcare professional to request that restraints not be used, and the requirement under subsection (b)(3)(B) to comply with such a request.

(2) DEVELOPMENT OF

GUIDELINES.-In developing the guidelines required by para- graph (1), the Directors shall each consult with healthcare professionals with expertise in caring for women during the period of pregnancy and postpartum recovery.

(g) Definitions.-For purposes of this section:

(1) POSTPARTUM RECOVERY.-The term 'postpartum recovery' means the 12-week period, or longer as determined by the healthcare professional responsible for the health and safety of the prisoner, following delivery, and shall include the entire period that the prisoner is in the hospital or infirmary.

(2) PRISONER.-The term 'prisoner' means a person who has been sentenced to a term of imprisonment pursuant to a conviction for a Federal criminal offense, or a person in the custody of the Bureau of Prisons, including a person in a Bureau of Prisons contracted facility.

(3) RESTRAINTS.-The term

'restraints' means any physical or mechanical device used to control the movement of a prisoner's body, limbs, or both.

(b) Clerical amendment.-The table of sections for chapter 317 of title 18, United States Code, is amended by adding after the item relating to section 4321 the following:

"**4322.** Use of restraints on prisoners during the period of pregnancy, labor, and postpartum recovery prohibited."

TITLE IV Sentencing Reform

SEC. 401. Reduce and restrict enhanced sentencing for prior drug felonies.

(a) Controlled Substances Act amendments.-The Controlled Substances Act (21 U.S.C. 801 et seq.) is amended-

(1) in section 102 **(21 U.S.C. 802)**, by adding at the end the following:

"**(57) The term 'serious drug**

felony' means an offense described in section 924(e)(2) of title 18, United States Code, for which-

(A) the offender served a term of imprisonment of more than 12 months; and

(B) the offender's release from any term of imprisonment was within 15 years of the commencement of the instant offense.

(58) The term 'serious violent felony' means-

(A) an offense described in section 3559(c)(2) of title 18, United States Code, for which the offender served a term of imprisonment of more than 12 months; and

(B) any offense that would be a felony violation of section 113 of title 18, United States Code, if the offense were committed in the special maritime and territorial jurisdiction of the United States, for which the offender served a term of imprisonment of more than 12 months."; and

(2) in section 401(b)(1) **(21 U.S.C. 841(b)(1))**-

(A) in subparagraph (A), in the matter following clause (viii)-

(i) by striking "If any person commits such a violation after a prior conviction for a felony drug offense has become final, such person shall be sentenced to a term of imprisonment which may not be less than 20 years" and inserting the following: "If any person commits such a violation after a prior conviction for a serious drug felony or serious violent felony has become final, such person shall be sentenced to a term of imprisonment of not less than 15 years"; and

(ii) by striking after two or more prior convictions for a felony drug offense have become final, such person shall be sentenced to a mandatory term of life imprisonment without release and inserting the following: after 2 or more prior convictions for a serious drug felony or serious violent felony have become final, such person shall be sentenced to a term of imprisonment of not less than 25 years; and

(B) in subparagraph (B), in the matter following clause (viii), by striking If any person commits such a violation after a prior conviction for a felony drug offense has become final and inserting the following: If any person commits such a violation after a prior conviction for a serious drug felony or serious violent felony has become final."

(b) Controlled Substances Import and Export Act amendments.-Section 1010(b) of the Controlled Substances Import and Export Act **(21 U.S.C. 960(b))** is amended-

(1) in paragraph (1), in the matter following subparagraph (H), by striking If any per- son commits such a violation after a prior conviction for a felony drug offense has become final, such person shall be sentenced to a term of imprisonment of not less than 20 years and inserting If any person commits such a violation after a prior conviction for a serious drug felony or serious violent felony has become final, such person shall be sentenced to a term of

imprisonment of not less than 15 years; and

(2) in paragraph (2), in the matter following subparagraph (H), by striking felony drug offense and inserting serious drug felony or serious violent felony.

(c) Applicability to pending cases.-This section, and the amendments made by this section, shall apply to any offense that was committed before the date of enactment of this Act, if a sentence for the offense has not been imposed as of such date of enactment.

SEC. 402. Broadening of existing safety valve.

(a) Amendments.-Section 3553 of title 18, United States Code, is amended-

(1) in subsection (f)-

(A) in the matter preceding paragraph (1)-

(i) by striking or section 1010 and

inserting , section 1010; and

(ii) by inserting , or section 70503 or 70506 of title 46 after 963);

(B) by striking paragraph (1) and inserting the following:

(1) the defendant does not have-

(A) more than 4 criminal history points, excluding any criminal history points resulting from a 1-point offense, as determined under the sentencing guidelines;

(B) a prior 3-point offense, as determined under the sentencing guidelines; and

(C) a prior 2-point violent offense, as determined under the sentencing guidelines; and

(1) by adding at the end the

following:

"Information disclosed by a defendant under this subsection may not be used to enhance the sentence of the defendant unless the information relates to a violent offense."; and

(2) by adding at the end the following:

"(g) Definition of violent offense.-As used in this section, the term 'violent offense' means a crime of violence, as defined in section 16, that is punishable by imprisonment."

(b) Applicability.- The amendments made by this section shall apply only to a conviction entered on or after the date of enactment of this Act.

SEC. 403. CLARIFICATION OF SECTION 924(c) OF TITLE 18, UNITED STATES CODE.

(a) In general.-Section 924(c)(1)(C) of title 18, United States Code, is amended, in the matter preceding clause (i), by striking second or subsequent conviction under this subsection and inserting violation of this subsection that occurs after a prior conviction under this subsection has become final.

(b) Applicability to pending cases.-This section, and the amendments made by this section, shall apply to any offense that was committed before the date of enactment of this Act, if a sentence for the offense has not been imposed as of such date of enactment.

SEC. 404. Application of Fair Sentencing Act.

(a) Definition of covered offense.-In this section, the term covered offense means a violation of a Federal criminal statute, the statutory penalties for which were modified by section 2 or 3 of the Fair Sentencing Act of 2010 (Public Law 111-220; 124 Stat. 2372), that was committed before August 3, 2010.

(b) Defendants previously sentenced.-A

court that imposed a sentence for a covered offense may, on motion of the defendant, the Director of the Bureau of Prisons, the attorney for the Government, or the court, impose a reduced sentence as if sections 2 and 3 of the Fair Sentencing Act of 2010 (Public Law 111-220; 124 Stat. 2372) were in effect at the time the covered offense was committed.

(c) Limitations.-No court shall entertain a motion made under this section to reduce a sentence if the sentence was previously imposed or previously reduced in accordance with the amendments made by sections 2 and 3 of the Fair Sentencing Act of 2010 (Public Law 111-220; 124 Stat. 2372) or if a previous motion made under this section to reduce the sentence was, after the date of enactment of this Act, denied after a complete review of the motion on the merits. Nothing in this section shall be construed to require a court to reduce any sentence pursuant to this section.

TITLE V Second Chance Act of 2007 reauthorization

SEC. 501. Short Title.

This title may be cited as the Second Chance Reauthorization Act of 2018. SEC. 502. Improvements to existing programs.

SEC. 502. Improvements To Existing Programs.

(a) Reauthorization of adult and juvenile offender State and local demonstration projects.-Section 2976 of title I of the Omnibus Crime Control and Safe Streets Act of 1968 **(34 U.S.C. 10631)** is amended-

(1) by striking subsection (a) and inserting the following:

"(a) Grant authorization.-The Attorney General shall make grants to States, local governments, territories, or Indian tribes, or any combination thereof (in this section referred to as an 'eligible entity'), in partnership with interested persons (including Federal corrections and supervision agencies), service providers, and nonprofit organizations for the purpose of strategic planning and implementation of adult and juvenile offender reentry projects.";

(2) in subsection (b)-

(A) in paragraph (3), by inserting or reentry courts, after community,;

(B) in paragraph (6), by striking and at the end;

(C) in paragraph (7), by striking the period at the end and inserting ; and; and

(D) by adding at the end the following:

"(8) promoting employment opportunities consistent with the Transitional Jobs strategy (as defined in section 4 of the Second Chance Act of 2007 **(34 U.S.C. 60502))**."; and

(3) by striking subsections (d), (e), and (f) and inserting the following:

"(d) Combined grant application; priority consideration.-

(1) IN GENERAL.-The Attorney General shall develop a procedure to allow applicants to submit a single application for a planning grant under subsection (e) and an implementation grant under subsection (f)."

(2) PRIORITY CONSIDERATION.-The Attorney General shall give priority consideration to grant applications under subsections (e) and (f) that include a commitment by the applicant to partner with a local evaluator to identify and analyze data that will-

(A) enable the grantee to target the intended offender population; and

(B) serve as a baseline for purposes of the evaluation.

(e) Planning grants.-

(1) IN GENERAL.-Except as provided in paragraph (3), the Attorney General may make a grant to an eligible entity of not more than $75,000 to develop a strategic, collaborative plan for an adult or juvenile offender reentry demonstration project as described in subsection (h) that includes-

(A) a budget and a budget justification;

(B) a description of the outcome measures that will be used to measure the effective- ness of the program in promoting public safety and public health;

(C) the activities proposed;

(D) a schedule for completion of the activities described in subparagraph (C); and

(E) a description of the personnel necessary to complete the activities described in sub- paragraph (C).

(2) MAXIMUM TOTAL GRANTS AND GEOGRAPHIC DIVERSITY.-

(A) MAXIMUM AMOUNT.-The Attorney General may not make initial planning grants and implementation grants to 1 eligible entity in a total amount that is more than a $1,000,000.

(B) GEOGRAPHIC DIVERSITY.-The Attorney General shall make every effort to ensure equitable geographic distribution of grants under this section and take into consideration the needs of underserved populations, including rural and tribal communities.

(3) PERIOD OF GRANT.-A planning grant made under this subsection shall be for a period of not longer than 1 year, beginning on the first day of the month in which the planning grant is made.

(f) Implementation grants.-

(1) APPLICATIONS.-An eligible entity desiring an implementation grant under this subsection shall submit to the Attorney General an application that-

(A) contains a reentry strategic plan as described in subsection (h), which describes the long-term strategy and incorporates a detailed implementation schedule, including the plans of the applicant to fund the program after Federal funding is discontinued;

(B) identifies the local government role and the role of governmental agencies and nonprofit organizations that will be coordinated by, and that will collaborate on, the offender reentry strategy of the applicant, and certifies the involvement of such agencies and organizations;

(C) describes the evidence-based methodology and outcome measures that will be used to evaluate the program funded with a grant under this subsection, and specifically explains how such measurements will provide valid measures of the impact of that pro- gram; and

(D) describes how the project could be broadly replicated if demonstrated to be effective.

(2) REQUIREMENTS.- The Attorney General may make a grant to an applicant under this subsection only if the application-

(A) reflects explicit support of the chief executive officer, or their designee, of the State, unit of local government, territory, or Indian tribe applying for a grant under this subsection;

(B) provides discussion of the role of Federal corrections, State corrections departments, community corrections agencies, juvenile justice systems, and tribal or local jail systems in ensuring successful reentry of offenders into their communities;

(C) provides evidence of collaboration with State, local, or tribal government agencies overseeing health, housing, child welfare, education, substance abuse, victims services, and employment services, and with local law enforcement agencies;

(D) provides a plan for analysis of the statutory, regulatory, rules-based, and practice- based hurdles to reintegration of offenders into the community;

(E) includes the use of a State, local, territorial, or tribal task force, described in sub- section (i), to carry out the activities funded under the grant;

(F) provides a plan for continued collaboration with a local evaluator as necessary to meeting the requirements under subsection (h); and

(G) demonstrates that the applicant participated in the planning grant process or engaged in comparable planning for the reentry project.

(3) PRIORITY CONSIDERATIONS.-The Attorney General shall give priority to grant applications under this subsection that best-

(A) focus initiative on geographic areas with a disproportionate population of offenders released from prisons, jails, and juvenile facilities;

(B) include-

(i) input from nonprofit organizations, in any case where relevant input is available and appropriate to the grant application;

(ii) consultation with crime victims and offenders who are released from prisons, jails, and juvenile facilities;

(iii) coordination with families of offenders;

(iv) input, where appropriate, from the juvenile justice coordinating council of the region;

(v) input, where appropriate, from the reentry coordinating council of the region; or

(vi) input, where appropriate, from other interested persons;

(C) demonstrate effective case assessment and management abilities in order to pro- vide comprehensive and continuous reentry, including-

(i) planning for

prerelease transitional housing and community release that begins upon admission for juveniles and jail inmates, and, as appropriate, for prison inmates, depending on the length of the sentence;

(ii) establishing prerelease planning procedures to ensure that the eligibility of an offender for Federal, tribal, or State benefits upon release is established prior to release, subject to any limitations in law, and to ensure that offenders obtain all necessary referrals for reentry services, including assistance identifying and securing suitable housing; or

(iii) delivery of continuous and appropriate mental health services, drug treatment, medical care, job training and placement, educational services, vocational services, and any other service or support needed for reentry;

(D) review the process by which the applicant adjudicates violations of parole, probation, or supervision following release from prison, jail, or a juvenile facility, taking into account public safety and the use of graduated, community-based sanctions for minor and technical violations of parole, probation, or supervision (specifically those violations that are not otherwise, and independently, a violation of law);

(E) provide for an independent evaluation of reentry programs that include, to the maximum extent possible, random assignment and controlled studies to determine the effectiveness of such programs;

(F) target moderate and high-risk offenders for reentry programs through validated assessment tools; or

(G) target offenders with histories of homelessness, substance abuse, or mental illness, including a prerelease assessment of the housing status of the offender and behavioral health needs of the offender with clear coordination with mental health, substance abuse, and homelessness services systems to achieve stable and permanent housing outcomes with appropriate support service.

(4) PERIOD OF GRANT.-A grant made under this subsection shall be effective for a 2-year period-

(A) beginning on the date on which the planning grant awarded under subsection (e) concludes; or

(B) in the case of an implementation grant awarded to an eligible entity that did not receive a planning grant, beginning on the date on which the implementation grant is awarded.;

(4) in subsection (h)-

(A) by redesignating paragraphs (2) and (3) as paragraphs (3) and (4), respectively; and

(B) by striking paragraph (1) and inserting the following:

(1) IN GENERAL.- As a condition of receiving financial assistance under subsection (f), each application shall develop a comprehensive reentry strategic plan that-

(A) contains a plan to assess inmate reentry needs and measurable annual and

3-year performance outcomes;

(B) uses, to the maximum extent possible, randomly assigned and controlled studies, or rigorous quasi-experimental studies with matched comparison groups, to determine the effectiveness of the program funded with a grant under subsection (f); and

(C) includes as a goal of the plan to reduce the rate of recidivism for offenders released from prison, jail or a juvenile facility with funds made available under subsection (f).

(2) LOCAL EVALUATOR.-A partnership with a local evaluator described in subsection (d)(2) shall require the local evaluator to use the baseline data and target population characteristics developed under a subsection (e) planning grant to derive a target goal for recidivism reduction during the 3-year period beginning on the date of implementation of the program.;

(5) in subsection (i)(1)-

(A) in the matter preceding subparagraph (A), by striking under this section and inserting under subsection (f); and

(B) in subparagraph (B), by striking subsection (e)(4) and inserting subsection (f)(2) (D);

(6) "in subsection (j)-

(A) in paragraph (1), by inserting for an implementation grant under subsection (f) after applicant;

(B) in paragraph (2)-

(i) in subparagraph (E), by inserting , where appropriate after support; and

(ii) by striking subparagraphs (F), (G), and (H), and inserting the following:

(F) increased number of staff trained to administer reentry services;

(G) increased proportion of individuals served by the program among those eligible to receive services;

(H) increased number of individuals receiving risk screening needs assessment, and case planning services;

(I) increased enrollment in, and completion of treatment services, including substance abuse and mental health services among those assessed as needing such services;

(J) increased enrollment in and degrees earned from educational programs, including high school, GED, vocational training, and college education;

(K) increased number of individuals obtaining and retaining employment;

(L) increased number of individuals obtaining and maintaining housing;

(M) increased self-reports of successful community living, including stability of living situation and positive family relationships;

(N) reduction in drug and alcohol use; and

(O) reduction in recidivism rates for individuals receiving reentry services after release, as compared to either baseline recidivism rates in the jurisdiction of the grantee or recidivism rates of the control or comparison group.";

(C) in paragraph (3), by striking facilities. and inserting facilities, including a cost- benefit analysis to determine the cost effectiveness of the reentry program.;

(D) in paragraph (4), by striking this section and inserting subsection (f); and

(E) in paragraph (5), by striking this section and inserting subsection (f);

(7) in subsection (k)(1), by striking this section each place the term appears and inserting subsection (f);

(8) in subsection (l)-

(A) in paragraph (2), by inserting beginning on the date on which the most recent implementation grant is made to the grantee under subsection (f) after 2-year period; and

(B) in paragraph (4), by striking over a 2-year period and inserting during the 2-year period described in paragraph (2);

(9) in subsection (o)(1), by striking appropriated and all that follows and inserting the following: appropriated $35,000,000 for each of fiscal years 2019 through 2023.; and

(10) by adding at the end the

following:

"(p) Definition.-In this section, the term 'reentry court' means a program that-

(1) monitors juvenile and adult eligible offenders reentering the community;

(2) provides continual judicial supervision;

(3) provides juvenile and adult eligible offenders reentering the community with coordinated and comprehensive reentry services and programs, such as-

(A) drug and alcohol testing and assessment for treatment;

(B) assessment for substance abuse from a substance abuse professional who is approved by the State or Indian tribe and licensed by the appropriate entity to provide alcohol and drug addiction treatment, as appropriate;

(C) substance abuse treatment, including medication assisted treatment, from a provider that is approved by the State or Indian tribe, and licensed, if necessary, to provide medical and other health services;

(D) health (including mental health) services and assessment; (E) aftercare and case management services that-

(i) facilitate access to clinical care and related health services; and

(ii) coordinate with such clinical care and related health services; and

(F) any other services needed for reentry;

(4) convenes community impact panels, victim impact panels, or victim impact

educational classes;

(5) provides and coordinates the delivery of community services to juvenile and adult eligible offenders, including-

(A) housing assistance;

(B) education;

(C) job training;

(D) conflict resolution skills training;

(E) batterer intervention programs; and

(F) other appropriate social services; and

(6) establishes and implements graduated sanctions and incentives..

(b) Grants for family-Based substance abuse treatment.- Part DD of title I of the Omnibus Crime Control and Safe Streets Act of 1968 **(34 U.S.C. 10591 et seq.)** is amended-

(1) in section 2921 **(34 U.S.C. 10591)**, in the matter preceding paragraph (1), by inserting nonprofit organizations, before and Indian;

(2) in section 2923 **(34 U.S.C. 10593)**, by adding at the end the following:

(c) Priority considerations.-The Attorney General shall give priority consideration to grant applications for grants under section 2921 that are submitted by a nonprofit organization that demonstrates a relationship with State and local criminal justice agencies, including-

(1) within the judiciary and prosecutorial agencies; or

(2) with the local corrections agencies, which shall be documented by a written agreement that details the terms of access to facilities and participants and provides information on the history of the organization of

working with correctional populations.; and

(3) by striking section 2926(a) and inserting the following:

(a) In general.-There are authorized to be appropriated to carry out this part $10,000,000 for each of fiscal years 2019 through 2023..

(c) Grant program To evaluate and improve educational methods at prisons, jails, and juvenile facilities.-Title I of the Omnibus Crime Control and Safe Streets Act of 1968 **(42 U.S.C. 3711 et seq.)** is amended-

(1) by striking the second part designated as part JJ, as added by the Second Chance Act of 2007 (Public Law 110-199; 122 Stat. 677), relating to grants to evaluate and improve educational methods at prisons, jails, and juvenile facilities;

(2) by adding at the end the following:

"PART NN-Grant program to evaluate

and improve educational methods at prisons, jails, and juvenile facilities."

SEC. 3041. Grant program to evaluate and improve educational methods at prisons, jails, and juvenile facilities.

(a) Grant program authorized.-The Attorney General may carry out a grant program under which the Attorney General may make grants to States, units of local government, territories, Indian Tribes, and other public and private entities to-

(1) evaluate methods to improve academic and vocational education for offenders in prisons, jails, and juvenile facilities;

(2) identify, and make recommendations to the Attorney General regarding, best practices relating to academic and vocational education for offenders in prisons, jails, and juvenile facilities, based on the evaluation under paragraph (1);

(3) improve the academic and

vocational education programs (including technology career training) available to offenders in prisons, jails, and juvenile facilities; and

(4) implement methods to improve academic and vocational education for offenders in prisons, jails, and juvenile facilities consistent with the best practices identified in sub- section (c).

(b) Application.-To be eligible for a grant under this part, a State or other entity described in subsection (a) shall submit to the Attorney General an application in such form and manner, at such time, and accompanied by such information as the Attorney General specifies.

(c) Best practices.-Not later than 180 days after the date of enactment of the Second Chance Reauthorization Act of 2018, the Attorney General shall identify and publish best practices relating to academic and vocational education for offenders in prisons, jails, and juvenile facilities. The best practices shall consider the evaluations performed and recommendations made under grants made under subsection (a) before the date of enactment of the Second Chance Reauthorization Act of 2018.

(d) Report.-Not later than 90 days after the last day of the final fiscal year of a grant under this part, each entity described in subsection (a) receiving such a grant shall submit to the Attorney General a detailed report of the progress made by the entity using such grant, to permit the Attorney General to evaluate and improve academic and vocational education methods carried out with grants under this part.; and

(3) in section 1001(a) of part J of title I of **the Omnibus Crime Control and Safe Streets Act of 1968 (34 U.S.C. 10261(a))**, by adding at the end the following:

"(28) There are authorized to be appropriated to carry out section 3031(a)(4) of part NN $5,000,000 for each of fiscal years 2019, 2020, 2021, 2022, and 2023."

(d) Careers training demonstration grants.-Section 115 of the Second Chance Act of 2007 **(34 U.S.C. 60511)** is amended-

(1) in the heading, by striking Technology careers and inserting Careers;

(2) in subsection (a)-

(A) by striking and Indian and inserting nonprofit organizations, and Indian; and

(B) by striking technology career training to prisoners and inserting career training, including subsidized employment, when part of a training program, to prisoners and reentering youth and adults;

(3) in subsection (b)-

(A) by striking technology careers training;

(B) by striking technology-based; and

(C) by inserting , as well as upon transition and reentry into the community after facility;

(4) by striking subsection (e);

(5) by redesignating subsections (c) and (d) as subsections (d) and (e), respectively;

(6) by inserting after subsection (b) the following:

(c) Priority consideration.-Priority consideration shall be given to any application under this section that-

(1) provides assessment of local demand for employees in the geographic areas to which offenders are likely to return;

(2) conducts individualized reentry career planning upon the start of incarceration or post-release employment planning for each offender served under the grant;

(3) demonstrates connections to employers within the local community; or

(4) tracks and monitors employment outcomes.; and

by adding at the end the following:

"(f) Authorization of appropriations.-There are authorized to be appropriated to carry out this section $10,000,000 for each of fiscal years 2019, 2020, 2021, 2022, and 2023."

(e) Offender reentry substance abuse and criminal justice collaboration program.-Section 201(f)(1) of the Second Chance Act of 2007 **(34 U.S.C. 60521(f)(1))** is amended to read as follows:

(1) IN GENERAL.-There are authorized to be appropriated to carry out this section $15,000,000 for each of fiscal years 2019 through 2023..

(f) Community-Based mentoring and

transitional service grants to nonprofit organizations.-

(1) IN GENERAL.-Section 211 of the **Second Chance Act of 2007 (34 U.S.C. 60531)** is amended-

(A) in the header, by striking Mentoring grants to nonprofit organizations and inserting Community-based mentoring and transitional service grants to nonprofit organizations;

(B) in subsection (a), by striking mentoring and other;

(C) in subsection (b), by striking paragraph (2) and inserting the following:

(2) transitional services to assist in the reintegration of offenders into the community, including-

(A) educational, literacy, and vocational, services and the Transitional Jobs strategy;

(B) substance abuse treatment and services;

(C) coordinated supervision and services for offenders, including physical health care and comprehensive housing and mental health care;

(D) family services; and

(E) validated assessment tools to assess the risk factors of returning inmates; and..

in subsection (f), by striking this section and all that follows and inserting the following: this section $15,000,000 for each of fiscal years 2019 through 2023.

(2) TABLE OF CONTENTS AMENDMENT.-The table of contents in section 2 of the Second Chance Act of 2007 (Public Law 110-199; 122 Stat. 657) is amended by striking the item relating to section 211 and inserting the following:

"Sec. 211. Community-based mentoring and transitional service grants."

(g) Definitions.-

(1) IN GENERAL.-Section 4 of the Second Chance Act of 2007 **(34 U.S.C. 60502)** is amended to read as follows:

SEC. 4. Definitions. In this Act-

(1) the term 'exoneree' means an individual who-

(A) has been convicted of a Federal, tribal, or State offense that is punishable by a term of imprisonment of more than 1 year;

(B) has served a term of imprisonment for not less than 6 months in a Federal, tribal, or State prison or correctional facility as a result of the conviction described in subparagraph (A); and

(C) has been determined to be factually innocent of the offense described in subparagraph (A);

(2) the term 'Indian tribe' has the meaning given in section 901 of title I of the Omni- bus Crime Control and Safe Streets Act of 1968 **(34 U.S.C. 10251)**;

(3) the term 'offender' includes an exoneree; and

(4) the term 'Transitional Jobs strategy' means an employment strategy for youth and adults who are chronically unemployed or those that have barriers to employment that-

(A) is conducted by State, tribal, and local governments, State, tribal, and local work- force boards, and nonprofit organizations;

(B) provides time-limited employment using individual placements, team placements, and social enterprise placements, without displacing existing employees;

(C) pays wages in accordance with applicable law, but in no event less than the higher of the rate specified in section 6(a)(1) of the Fair Labor Standards Act of 1938 **(29 U.S.C. 206(a)(1))** or the applicable State or local minimum wage law, which are subsidized, in whole or in part, by public funds;

(D) combines time-limited employment with activities that promote skill development, remove barriers to employment, and lead to unsubsidized employment such as a thorough orientation and individual assessment, job readiness and life skills training, case management and supportive services, adult education and training, child support-related services, job retention support and incentives, and other similar activities;

(E) places participants into unsubsidized employment; and

(F) provides job retention, re-employment services, and continuing and vocational edu- cation to ensure continuing participation in unsubsidized employment and identification of opportunities for advancement..

(2) TABLE OF CONTENTS AMENDMENT.-The table of contents in section 2 of the Second Chance Act of 2007 (Public Law 110-199; 122 Stat. 657) is amended by striking the item relating to section 4 and inserting the following:

Sec. 4. Definitions..

(h) Extension of the length of section 2976 grants.-Section 6(1) of the Second Chance Act of 2007 **(34 U.S.C. 60504(1))** is amended by inserting or under section 2976 of the Omnibus Crime Control and Safe Streets Act of 1968 **(34 U.S.C. 10631)** after and 212.

SEC. 503. Audit and accountability of grantees.

(a) Definitions. In this section -

(1) the term covered grant program means grants awarded under section 115, 201, or 211 of the Second Chance Act of 2007 **(34**

U.S.C. 60511, 60521, and 60531), as amended by this title;

(2) the term covered grantee means a recipient of a grant from a covered grant program;

(3) the term nonprofit, when used with respect to an organization, means an organization that is described in section 501(c)(3) of the Internal Revenue Code of 1986, and is exempt from taxation under section 501(a) of such Code; and

(4) the term unresolved audit finding means an audit report finding in a final audit report of the Inspector General of the Department of Justice that a covered grantee has used grant funds awarded to that grantee under a covered grant program for an unauthorized expenditure or otherwise unallowable cost that is not closed or resolved during a 12-month period prior to the date on which the final audit report is issued.

(b) Audit requirement.-Beginning in fiscal

year 2019, and annually thereafter, the Inspector General of the Department of Justice shall conduct audits of covered grantees to prevent waste, fraud, and abuse of funds awarded under covered grant programs. The Inspector General shall determine the appropriate number of covered grantees to be audited each year.

(c) Mandatory exclusion.-A grantee that is found to have an unresolved audit finding under an audit conducted under subsection (b) may not receive grant funds under a covered grant program in the fiscal year following the fiscal year to which the finding relates.

(d) Reimbursement.-If a covered grantee is awarded funds under the covered grant program from which it received a grant award during the 1-fiscal-year period during which the covered grantee is ineligible for an allocation of grant funds under subsection (c), the Attorney General shall-

(1) deposit into the General Fund of the Treasury an amount that is equal to the amount of the grant funds that were improperly

awarded to the covered grantee; and

(2) seek to recoup the costs of the repayment to the Fund from the covered grantee that was improperly awarded the grant funds.

(e) Priority of grant awards.-The Attorney General, in awarding grants under a covered grant program shall give priority to eligible entities that during the 2-year period pre- ceding the application for a grant have not been found to have an unresolved audit finding.

(f) Nonprofit requirements.-

(1) PROHIBITION.-A nonprofit organization that holds money in offshore accounts for the purpose of avoiding the tax described in section 511(a) of the Internal Revenue Code of 1986, shall not be eligible to receive, directly or indirectly, any funds from a covered grant program.

(2) DISCLOSURE.-Each nonprofit organization that is a covered grantee shall disclose in its application for such a grant, as a

condition of receipt of such a grant, the compensation of its officers, directors, and trustees. Such disclosure shall include a description of the criteria relied on to determine such compensation.

(g) Prohibition on lobbying activity.-

(1) IN GENERAL.-Amounts made available under a covered grant program may not be used by any covered grantee to-

(A) lobby any representative of the Department of Justice regarding the award of grant funding; or

(B) lobby any representative of the Federal Government or a State, local, or tribal government regarding the award of grant funding.

(2) PENALTY.-If the Attorney General determines that a covered grantee has violated paragraph (1), the Attorney General shall-

(A) require the covered grantee to repay the grant in full; and

(B) prohibit the covered grantee from receiving a grant under the covered grant pro- gram from which it received a grant award during at least the 5-year period beginning on the date of such violation.

SEC. 504. FEDERAL REENTRY IMPROVEMENTS.

(a) Responsible reintegration of offenders.-Section 212 of the Second Chance Act of 2007 **(34 U.S.C. 60532)** is repealed.

(b) Federal prisoner reentry initiative.-Section 231 of the Second Chance Act of 2007 **(34 U.S.C. 60541)** is amended-

(1) in subsection (g)-

(A) in paragraph (3), by striking carried out during fiscal years 2009 and 2010 and inserting carried out during fiscal years 2019 through 2023; and

(B) in paragraph (5)(A)(ii), by striking the greater of 10 years or;

(2) by striking subsection (h);

(3) by redesignating subsection (i) as subsection (h); and

(4) in subsection (h), as so redesignated, by striking 2009 and 2010 and inserting 2019 through 2023.

(c) Enhancing reporting requirements pertaining to community corrections.-Section 3624(c) of title 18, United States Code, is amended-

(1) in paragraph (5), in the second sentence, by inserting , and number of prisoners not being placed in community corrections facilities for each reason set forth before , and any other information; and

(2) in paragraph (6), by striking the Second Chance Act of 2007 and inserting the Second Chance Reauthorization Act of 2018.

(d) Termination of study on effectiveness of depot naltrexone for heroin addiction.

Section 244 of the Second Chance Act of 2007 **(34 U.S.C. 60554)** is repealed.

(e) Authorization of appropriations for research.-Section 245 of the Second Chance Act of 2007 **(34 U.S.C. 60555)** is amended-

(1) by striking 243, and 244 and inserting and 243; and

(2) by striking $10,000,000 for each of the fiscal years 2009 and 2010 and inserting $5,000,000 for each of the fiscal years 2019, 2020, 2021, 2022, and 2023.

(f) Federal prisoner recidivism reduction programming enhancement.-

(1) IN GENERAL.-Section 3621 of title 18, United States Code, as amended by section 102(a) of this Act, is amended-

(A) by redesignating

subsection (g) as subsection (i); and

(B) by inserting after subsection (f) the following:

"(g) Partnerships To expand access to reentry programs proven To reduce recidivism.-

(1) DEFINITION.-The term 'demonstrated to reduce recidivism' means that the Director of Bureau of Prisons has determined that appropriate research has been conducted and has validated the effectiveness of the type of program on recidivism.

(2) ELIGIBILITY FOR RECIDIVISM REDUCTION PARTNERSHIP.-A faith-based or community-based nonprofit organization that provides mentoring or other programs that have been demonstrated to reduce recidivism is eligible to enter into a recidivism reduction partnership with a prison or community-based facility operated by the Bureau of Prisons.

(3) RECIDIVISM REDUCTION PARTNERSHIPS.-The Director of the Bureau of Prisons shall develop policies to require wardens of prisons and community-based facilities to enter into recidivism reduction partnerships with faith-based and community-based nonprofit organizations that are willing to provide, on a volunteer basis, programs described in paragraph (2).

(4) REPORTING REQUIREMENT.-The Director of the Bureau of Prisons shall submit to Congress an annual report on the last day of each fiscal year that-

(A) details, for each prison and community-based facility for the fiscal year just ended-

(i) the number of recidivism reduction partnerships under this section that were in effect;

(ii) the number of volunteers that provided recidivism reduction programming; and

(iii) the number of recidivism reduction programming hours provided; and

(B) explains any disparities between facilities in the numbers reported under subparagraph (A).

(2) EFFECTIVE DATE.-The amendments made by paragraph (1) shall take effect 180 days after the date of enactment of this Act."

(g) Repeals.-

(1) Section 2978 of title I of the Omnibus Crime Control and Safe Streets Act of 1968 **(34 U.S.C. 10633)** is repealed.

(2) Part CC of title I of the Omnibus Crime Control and Safe Streets Act of 1968 **(34 U.S.C. 10581 et seq.)** is repealed.

SEC. 505. Federal interagency reentry coordination.

(a) Reentry coordination.-The Attorney General, in consultation with the Secretary of Housing and Urban Development, the Secretary of Labor, the Secretary of Education, the Secretary of Health and Human Services, the Secretary of Veterans Affairs, the Secretary of Agriculture, and the heads of such other agencies of the Federal Government as the Attorney General considers appropriate, and in collaboration with interested persons, service providers, nonprofit organizations, and State, tribal, and local governments, shall coordinate on Federal programs, policies, and activities relating to the reentry of individuals returning from incarceration to the community, with an emphasis on evidence-based practices and protection against duplication of services.

(b) Report.-Not later than 2 years after the

date of the enactment of this Act, the Attorney General, in consultation with the Secretaries listed in subsection (a), shall submit to Congress a report summarizing the achievements under subsection (a), and including recommendations for Congress that would further reduce barriers to successful reentry.

SEC. 506. CONFERENCE EXPENDITURES.

(a) Limitation.-No amounts authorized to be appropriated to the Department of Justice under this title, or any amendments made by this title, may be used by the Attorney General, or by any individual or organization awarded discretionary funds under this title, or any amendments made by this title, to host or support any expenditure for conferences that uses more than $20,000 in Department funds, unless the Deputy Attorney General or such Assistant Attorney Generals, Directors, or principal deputies as the Deputy Attorney General may designate, provides prior written authorization that the funds may be expended to host a conference. A conference that uses more than $20,000 in such funds, but less than an average of $500 in such funds for each attendee of the conference, shall not be subject to the limitations of this section.

(b) Written approval.-Written approval under subsection (a) shall include a written estimate of all costs associated with the conference, including the cost of all food and beverages, audiovisual equipment, honoraria for speakers, and any entertainment.

(c) Report.-The Deputy Attorney General shall submit an annual report to the Commit- tee on the Judiciary of the Senate and the Committee on the Judiciary of the House of Representatives on all approved conference expenditures referenced in this section.

SEC. 507. Evaluation of the Second Chance Act program.

SEC. 507. EVALUATION OF THE SECOND CHANCE ACT PROGRAM.

(a) Evaluation of the second chance act

grant program.- Not later than 5 years after the date of enactment of this Act, the National Institute of Justice shall evaluate the effectiveness of grants used by the Department of Justice to support offender reentry and recidivism reduction programs at the State, local, Tribal, and Federal levels. The National Institute of Justice shall evaluate the following:

(1) The effectiveness of such programs in relation to their cost, including the extent to which the programs improve reentry outcomes, including employment, education, housing, reductions in recidivism, of participants in comparison to comparably situated individuals who did not participate in such programs and activities.

(2) The effectiveness of program structures and mechanisms for delivery of services.

(3) The impact of such programs on the communities and participants involved.

(4) The impact of such programs on

related programs and activities.

(5) The extent to which such programs meet the needs of various demographic groups.

(6) The quality and effectiveness of technical assistance provided by the Department of Justice to grantees for implementing such programs.

(7) Such other factors as may be appropriate.

(b) Authorization of funds for evaluation.-Not more than 1 percent of any amounts authorized to be appropriated to carry out the Second Chance Act grant program shall be made available to the National Institute of Justice each year to evaluate the processes, implementation, outcomes, costs, and effectiveness of the Second Chance Act grant program in improving reentry and reducing recidivism. Such funding may be used to provide support to grantees for supplemental data collection, analysis, and coordination associated with evaluation activities.

(c) Techniques.-Evaluations conducted under this section shall use appropriate methodology and research designs. Impact evaluations conducted under this section shall include the use of intervention and control groups chosen by random assignment methods, to the extent possible.

(d) Metrics and Outcomes for Evaluation.-

(1) IN GENERAL.-Not later than 180 days after the date of enactment of this Act, the National Institute of Justice shall consult with relevant stakeholders and identify outcome measures, including employment, housing, education, and public safety, that are to be achieved by programs authorized under the Second Chance Act grant program and the metrics by which the achievement of such outcomes shall be determined.

(2) PUBLICATION.-Not later

than 30 days after the date on which the National Institute of Justice identifies metrics and outcomes under paragraph (1), the Attorney General shall publish such metrics and outcomes identified.

(e) Data collection.-As a condition of award under the Second Chance Act grant program (including a subaward under section 3021(b) of title I of the Omnibus Crime Control and Safe Streets Act of 1968 **(34 U.S.C. 10701(b)))**, grantees shall be required to collect and report to the Department of Justice data based upon the metrics identified under subsection (d). In accordance with applicable law, collection of individual-level data under a pledge of confidentiality shall be protected by the National Institute of Justice in accordance with such pledge.

(f) Data accessibility.-Not later than 5 years after the date of enactment of this Act, the National Institute of Justice shall-

(1) make data collected during the course of evaluation under this section available

in de-identified form in such a manner that reasonably protects a pledge of confidentiality to participants under subsection (e); and

(2) make identifiable data collected during the course of evaluation under this section available to qualified researchers for future research and evaluation, in accordance with applicable law.

(g) Publication and reporting of evaluation findings.-The National Institute of Justice shall-

(1) not later than 365 days after the date on which the enrollment of participants in an impact evaluation is completed, publish an interim report on such evaluation;

(2) not later than 90 days after the date on which any evaluation is completed, publish and make publicly available such evaluation; and

(3) not later than 60 days after the completion date described in paragraph (2), submit a report to the Committee on the

Judiciary of the House of Representatives and the Committee on the Judiciary of the Senate on such evaluation.

(h) Second Chance Act grant program defined.-In this section, the term Second Chance Act grant program means any grant program reauthorized under this title and the amendments made by this title.

SEC. 508. GAO REVIEW.

Not later than 3 years after the date of enactment of the First Step Act of 2018 the Comptroller General of the United States shall conduct a review of all of the grant awards made under this title and amendments made by this title that includes-

(1) an evaluation of the effectiveness of the reentry programs funded by grant awards under this title and amendments made by this title at reducing recidivism, including a determination of which reentry programs were most effective;

(2) recommendations on how to improve the effectiveness of reentry programs, including those for which prisoners may earn time credits under the First Step Act of 2018; and

(3) an evaluation of the effectiveness of mental health services, drug treatment, medical care, job training and placement, educational services, and vocational services programs funded under this title and amendments made by this title.

TITLE VI Miscellaneous criminal justice

SEC. 601. Placement of prisoners close to families.

Section 3621(b) of title 18, United States Code, is amended-

(1) by striking shall designate the place of the prisoner's imprisonment. and inserting shall designate the place of the prisoner's imprisonment, and shall, subject to bed availability, the prisoner's security

designation, the prisoner's programmatic needs, the prisoner's mental and medical health needs, any request made by the prisoner related to faith-based needs, recommendations of the sentencing court, and other security concerns of the Bureau of Prisons, place the prisoner in a facility as close as practicable to the prisoner's primary residence, and to the extent practicable, in a facility within 500 driving miles of that residence. The Bureau shall, subject to consideration of the factors described in the preceding sentence and the prisoner's preference for staying at his or her current facility or being transferred, transfer prisoners to facilities that are closer   to the prisoner's primary residence even if the prisoner is already in a facility within 500 driving miles of that residence.; and

(2) by adding at the end the following: Notwithstanding any other provision of law, a designation of a place of imprisonment under this subsection is not reviewable by any court..

SEC. 602. Home confinement for low-risk prisoners.

Section 3624(c)(2) of title 18, United States Code, is amended by adding at the end the following: The Bureau of Prisons shall, to the extent practicable, place prisoners with lower risk levels and lower needs on home confinement for the maximum amount of time permitted under this paragraph.

SEC. 603. Federal prisoner reentry initiative reauthorization; modification of imposed term of imprisonment.

(a) Federal prisoner reentry initiative reauthorization.-Section 231(g) of the Second Chance Act of 2007 **(34 U.S.C. 60541(g))** is amended-

(1) in paragraph (1)-

(A) by inserting and eligible terminally ill offenders after elderly offenders each place the term appears;

(B) in subparagraph (A), by striking a Bureau of Prisons facility and inserting Bureau of Prisons facilities;

(C) in subparagraph (B)-

(i) by striking the Bureau of Prisons facility and inserting Bureau of Prisons facilities; and

(ii) by inserting , upon written request from either the Bureau of Prisons or an eligible elderly offender or eligible terminally ill offender after to home detention; and

(D) in subparagraph (C), by striking the Bureau of Prisons facility and inserting Bureau of Prisons facilities;

(2) in paragraph (2), by inserting or eligible terminally ill offender after elderly offender;

(3) in paragraph (3), as amended by section 504(b)(1)(A) of this Act, by striking at least one Bureau of Prisons facility and inserting Bureau of Prisons facilities; and

(4) in paragraph (4)-

(A) by inserting or eligible terminally ill offender after each eligible elderly offender; and

(B) by inserting and eligible terminally ill offenders after eligible elderly offenders; and

(5) in paragraph (5)-

(A) in subparagraph (A)-

(i) in clause (i), striking 65 years of age and inserting 60 years of age; and

(ii) in clause (ii), as amended by section

504(b)(1)(B) of this Act, by striking 75 percent and inserting 2/3 ; and

(B) by adding at the end the following:

"(D) ELIGIBLE TERMINALLY ILL OFFENDER.-The term 'eligible terminally ill offender' means an offender in the custody of the Bureau of Prisons who-

(i) is serving a term of imprisonment based on conviction for an offense or offenses that do not include any crime of violence (as defined in section 16(a) of title 18, United States Code), sex offense (as defined in section 111(5) of the Sex Offender

Registration and Notification Act **(34 U.S.C. 20911(5)))**, offense described in section 2332b(g)(5)(B) of title 18, United States Code, or offense under chapter 37 of title 18, United States Code;

(ii) satisfies the criteria specified in clauses (iii) through (vii) of subparagraph (A); and

(iii) has been determined by a medical doctor approved by the Bureau of Prisons to be-

> (I) in need of care at a nursing home,

intermediate care facility, or assisted living facility, as those terms are defined in section 232 of the National Housing Act **(12 U.S.C. 1715w)**; or

(II) diagnosed with a terminal illness."

(b) Increasing the use and transparency of compassionate release.- Section 3582 of title 18, United States Code, is amended-

(1) in subsection (c)(1)(A), in the matter preceding clause (i), by inserting after Bureau of Prisons, the following: or upon motion of the defendant after the defendant has fully exhausted all administrative rights to appeal a failure of the Bureau of Prisons to bring

a motion on the defendant's behalf or the lapse of 30 days from the receipt of such a request by the warden of the defendant's facility, whichever is earlier,;

(2) by redesignating subsection (d) as subsection (e); and

(3) by inserting after subsection (c) the following:

(d) Notification requirements.-

(1) TERMINAL ILLNESS DEFINED.-In this subsection, the term 'terminal illness' means a disease or condition with an end-of-life trajectory.

(2) NOTIFICATION.-The Bureau of Prisons shall, subject to any applicable confidentiality requirements-

(A) in the case of a defendant diagnosed with a terminal illness-

(i) not later than 72

hours after the diagnosis notify the defendant's attorney, partner, and family members of the defendant's condition and inform the defendant's attorney, partner, and family members that they may prepare and submit on the defendant's behalf a request for a sentence reduction pursuant to subsection (c)(1)(A);

(ii) not later than 7 days after the date of the diagnosis, provide the defendant's partner and family members (including extended family) with an opportunity to visit the defendant in person;

(iii) upon request from the defendant or his attorney, partner, or a family member, ensure that Bureau of Prisons employees assist the defendant in the preparation, drafting, and submission of a request for a sentence reduction pursuant to subsection (c)(1) (A); and

(iv) not later than 14 days of receipt of a request for a sentence reduction submitted on the defendant's behalf by the defendant or the defendant's attorney, partner, or family member, process the request;

(B) in the case of a defendant

who is physically or mentally unable to submit a request for a sentence reduction pursuant to subsection (c)(1)(A)-

> (i) inform the defendant's attorney, partner, and family members that they may prepare and submit on the defendant's behalf a request for a sentence reduction pursuant to subsection (c)(1)(A);
>
> (ii) accept and process a request for sentence reduction that has been prepared and submitted on the defendant's behalf by the defendant's attorney, partner, or family member under clause (i); and
>
> (iii) upon request from

the defendant or his attorney, partner, or family member, ensure that Bureau of Prisons employees assist the defendant in the preparation, drafting, and submission of a request for a sentence reduction pursuant to subsection (c)(1) (A); and

(C) ensure that all Bureau of Prisons facilities regularly and visibly post, including in prisoner handbooks, staff training materials, and facility law libraries and medical and hospice facilities, and make available to prisoners upon demand, notice of-

(i) a defendant's ability to request a sentence reduction pursuant to subsection (c)(1) (A);

(ii) the procedures and

timelines for initiating and resolving requests described in clause (i); and

(iii) the right to appeal a denial of a request described in clause (i) after all administrative rights to appeal within the Bureau of Prisons have been exhausted.

(3) ANNUAL REPORT.- Not later than 1 year after the date of enactment of this subsection, and once every year thereafter, the Director of the Bureau of Prisons shall submit to the Committee on the Judiciary of the Senate and the Committee on the Judiciary of the House of Representatives a report on requests for sentence reductions pursuant to subsection (c)(1)(A), which shall include a description of, for the previous year-

(A) the number of prisoners

granted and denied sentence reductions, categorized by the criteria relied on as the grounds for a reduction in sentence;

(B) the number of requests initiated by or on behalf of prisoners, categorized by the criteria relied on as the grounds for a reduction in sentence;

(C) the number of requests that Bureau of Prisons employees assisted prisoners in drafting, preparing, or submitting, categorized by the criteria relied on as the grounds for a reduction in sentence, and the final decision made in each request;

(D) the number of requests that attorneys, partners, or family members submitted on a defendant's behalf, categorized by the criteria relied on as the grounds for a reduction in sentence, and the final decision made in each request;

(E) the number of requests approved by the Director of the Bureau of Prisons, categorized by the criteria relied on as the grounds for a reduction in sentence;

(F) the number of requests denied by the Director of the Bureau of Prisons and the rea- sons given for each denial, categorized by the criteria relied on as the grounds for a reduction in sentence;

(G) for each request, the time elapsed between the date the request was received by the warden and the final decision, categorized by the criteria relied on as the grounds for a reduction in sentence;

(H) for each request, the number of prisoners who died while their request was pending and, for each, the amount of time that had elapsed between the date the request was received by the Bureau of Prisons, categorized by the criteria relied on as the grounds for a reduction in sentence;

(I) the number of Bureau of Prisons notifications to attorneys, partners, and family members of their right to visit a terminally ill defendant as required under paragraph (2)(A)(ii) and, for each, whether a visit occurred and how much time elapsed between the notification and the visit;

(J) the number of visits to terminally ill prisoners that were denied by the Bureau of Prisons due to security or other concerns, and the reasons given for each denial; and

(K) the number of motions filed by defendants with the court after all administrative rights to appeal a denial of a sentence reduction had been exhausted, the outcome of each motion, and the time that had elapsed between the date the request was first received by the Bureau of Prisons and the date the defendant filed the motion with the court..

SEC. 604. Identification for returning citizens.

(a) Identification and release assistance for Federal prisoners.-Section 231(b) of the Second Chance Act of 2007 **(34 U.S.C. 60541(b))** is amended-

(1) in paragraph (1)-

(A) by striking (including and inserting prior to release from a term of imprisonment in a Federal prison or if the individual was not sentenced to a term of imprisonment in a Federal prison, prior to release from a sentence to a term in community confinement, including; and

(B) by striking or birth certificate) prior to release and inserting and a birth certificate; and

(2) by adding at the end the following:

"(4) DEFINITION.-In this subsection, the term 'community confinement' means residence in a community treatment center, halfway house, restitution center, mental health facility, alcohol or drug rehabilitation center, or other community facility."

(b) Duties of the Bureau of Prisons.-

Section 4042(a) of title 18, United States Code, is amended-

(1) by redesignating paragraphs (D) and (E) as paragraphs (6) and (7), respectively;

(2) in paragraph (6) (as so redesignated)-

(A) in clause (i)-

(i) by striking Social Security Cards,; and

(ii) by striking and at the end;

(B) by redesignating clause (ii) as clause (iii);

(C) by inserting after clause (i) the following:

(ii) obtain identification, including a social

security card, driver's license or other official photo identification, and a birth certificate; and;

(D) in clause (iii) (as so redesignated), by inserting after prior to release the following: from a sentence to a term of imprisonment in a Federal prison or if the individual was not sentenced to a term of imprisonment in a Federal prison, prior to release from a sentence to a term of community confinement; and

(E) by redesignating clauses (i), (ii), and (iii) (as so amended) as subparagraphs (A), (B), and (C), respectively, and adjusting the margins accordingly; and

(3) in paragraph (7) (as so redesignated), by redesignating clauses (i) through (vii) as subparagraphs (A) through (G), respectively, and adjusting the margins accordingly.

SEC. 605. Expanding inmate employment through Federal Prison Industries.

(a) New market authorizations.-Chapter 307 of title 18, United States Code, is amended by inserting after section 4129 the following:

(a) In general.-Except as provided in subsection (b), notwithstanding any other provision of law, Federal Prison Industries may sell products to-

(1) public entities for use in penal or correctional institutions;

(2) public entities for use in disaster relief or emergency response;

(3) the government of the District of Columbia; and

(4) any organization described in subsection (c)(3), (c)(4), or (d) of section 501 of the Internal Revenue Code of 1986 that is exempt from taxation under section 501(a) of such Code.

(b) Office furniture.- Federal Prison Industries may not sell office furniture to the organizations described in subsection (a)(4).

(c) Definitions.-In this section:

(1) The term 'office furniture' means any product or service offering intended to meet the furnishing needs of the workplace, including office, healthcare, educational, and hospitality environments.

(2) The term 'public entity' means a State, a subdivision of a State, an Indian tribe, and an agency or governmental corporation or business of any of the foregoing.

(3) The term 'State' means a State, the District of Columbia, the Commonwealth of Puerto Rico, Guam, American Samoa, the Northern Mariana Islands, and the United States Virgin Islands..

(b) Technical amendment.-The table of sections for chapter 307 of title 18, United States Code, is amended by inserting after the item relating to section 4129 the following:

4130. Additional markets.

(c) Deferred compensation.-Section 4126(c)(4) of title 18, United States Code, is amended by inserting after operations, the following: not less than 15 percent of such compensation for any inmate shall be reserved in the fund or a separate account and made available to assist the inmate with costs associated with release from prison;

(d) GAO report.-Beginning not later than 90 days after the date of enactment of this Act, the Comptroller General of the United States shall conduct an audit of Federal Prison Industries that includes the following:

(1) An evaluation of Federal Prison Industries's effectiveness in reducing recidivism compared to other rehabilitative programs in the prison system.

(2) An evaluation of the scope and size of the additional markets made available to

Federal Prison Industries under this section and the total market value that would be opened up to Federal Prison Industries for competition with private sector providers of products and services.

(3) An evaluation of whether the following factors create an unfair competitive environment between Federal Prison Industries and private sector providers of products and services which would be exacerbated by further expansion:

(A) Federal Prison Industries's status as a mandatory source of supply for Federal agencies and the requirement that the buying agency must obtain a waiver in order to make a competitive purchase from the private sector if the item to be acquired is listed on the schedule of products and services published by Federal Prison Industries.

(B) Federal Prison Industries's ability to determine that the price to be paid by Federal Agencies is fair and reasonable, rather than such a determination being made by the buying agency.

(C) An examination of the extent to which Federal Prison Industries is bound by the requirements of the generally applicable Federal Acquisition Regulation pertaining to the conformity of the delivered product with the specified design and performance specifications and adherence to the delivery schedule required by the Federal agency, based on the transactions being categorized as interagency transfers.

(D) An examination of the extent to which Federal Prison Industries avoids transactions that are little more than pass through transactions where the work provided by inmates does not create meaningful value or meaningful work opportunities for inmates.

(E) The extent to which Federal Prison Industries must comply with the same worker protection, workplace safety and similar regulations applicable to, and enforceable against, Federal contractors.

(F) The wages Federal Prison Industries pays to inmates, taking into account inmate productivity and other factors such as security concerns associated with having a facility in a prison.

(G) The effect of any additional cost advantages Federal Prison Industries has over private sector providers of goods and services, including-

>(i) the costs absorbed by the Bureau of Prisons such as inmate medical care and infrastructure expenses including real estate and utilities; and

>(ii) its exemption from Federal and State income taxes and property taxes.

(4) An evaluation of the extent to which the customers of Federal Prison Industries are satisfied with quality, price, and timely delivery of the products and services provided it

provides, including summaries of other independent assessments such as reports of agency inspectors general, if applicable.

SEC. 606. DE-ESCALATION TRAINING.

Beginning not later than 1 year after the date of enactment of this Act, the Director of the Bureau of Prisons shall incorporate into training programs provided to officers and employees of the Bureau of Prisons (including officers and employees of an organization with which the Bureau of Prisons has a contract to provide services relating to imprisonment) specialized and comprehensive training in procedures to-

(1) de-escalate encounters between a law enforcement officer or an officer or employee of the Bureau of Prisons, and a civilian or a prisoner (as such term is defined in section 3635 of title 18, United States Code, as added by section 101(a) of this Act); and

(2) identify and appropriately respond to incidents that involve the unique

needs of individuals who have a mental illness or cognitive deficit.

SEC. 607. Evidence-Based treatment for opioid and heroin abuse.

(a) Report on evidence-based treatment for opioid and heroin abuse.-Not later than 90 days after the date of enactment of this Act, the Director of the Bureau of Prisons shall submit to the Committees on the Judiciary and the Committees on Appropriations of the Senate and of the House of Representatives a report assessing the availability of and the capacity of the Bureau of Prisons to treat heroin and opioid abuse through evidence- based programs, including medication-assisted treatment where appropriate. In preparing the report, the Director shall consider medication-assisted treatment as a strategy to assist in treatment where appropriate and not as a replacement for holistic and other drug-free approaches. The report shall include a description of plans to expand access to evidence-based treatment for heroin and opioid abuse for prisoners, including access to medication-assisted treatment in appropriate cases. Following submission, the Director shall take steps to implement these plans.

(b) Report on the availability of medication-Assisted treatment for opioid and heroin abuse, and implementation thereof.-Not later than 120 days after the date of enactment of this Act, the Director of the Administrative Office of the United States Courts shall submit to the Committees on the Judiciary and the Committees on Appropriations of the Senate and of the House of Representatives a report assessing the availability of and capacity for the provision of medication assisted treatment for opioid and heroin abuse by treatment service providers serving prisoners who are serving a term of supervised release, and including a description of plans to expand access to medication-assisted treatment for heroin and opioid abuse whenever appropriate among prisoners under supervised release. Following submission, the Director will take steps to implement these plans.

SEC. 608. PILOT PROGRAMS.

(a) In general.- The Bureau of Prisons shall establish each of the following pilot programs for 5 years, in at least 20 facilities:

(1) MENTORSHIP FOR YOUTH.-A program to pair youth with volunteers from faith- based or community organizations, which may include formerly incarcerated offenders, that have relevant experience or expertise in mentoring, and a willingness to serve as a mentor in such a capacity.

(2) SERVICE TO ABANDONED, RESCUED, OR OTHERWISE VULNERABLE ANIMALS.-A program to equip prisoners with the skills to provide training and therapy to animals seized by Federal law enforcement under asset forfeiture authority and to organizations that provide shelter and similar services to abandoned, rescued, or otherwise vulnerable animals.

(b) Reporting requirement.-Not later than 1 year after the conclusion of the pilot programs, the Attorney General shall report to

Congress on the results of the pilot pro- grams under this section. Such report shall include cost savings, numbers of participants, and information about recidivism rates among participants.

(c) Definition.-In this title, the term youth means a prisoner (as such term is defined in section 3635 of title 18, United States Code, as added by section 101(a) of this Act) who was 21 years of age or younger at the time of the commission or alleged commission of the criminal offense for which the individual is being prosecuted or serving a term of imprisonment, as the case may be.

SEC. 609. Ensuring supervision of released sexually dangerous persons.

(a) Probation officers.-Section 3603 of title 18, United States Code, is amended in paragraph (8)(A) by striking or 4246 and inserting , 4246, or 4248.

(b) Pretrial services officers.-Section 3154 of title 18, United States Code, is amended in paragraph (12)(A) by striking or 4246 and inserting , 4246, or 4248.

SEC. 610. DATA COLLECTION.

(a) National Prisoner Statistics Program.-Beginning not later than 1 year after the date of enactment of this Act, and annually thereafter, pursuant to the authority under section 302 of the Omnibus Crime Control and Safe Streets Act of 1968 **(42 U.S.C. 3732)**, the Director of the Bureau of Justice Statistics, with information that shall be provided by the Director of the Bureau of Prisons, shall include in the National Prisoner Statistics Program the following:

(1) The number of prisoners (as such term is defined in section 3635 of title 18, United States Code, as added by section 101(a) of this Act) who are veterans of the Armed Forces of the United States.

(2) The number of prisoners who have been placed in solitary confinement at any time during the previous year.

(3) The number of female prisoners known by the Bureau of Prisons to be pregnant, as well as the outcomes of such pregnancies, including information on pregnancies that result in live birth, stillbirth, miscarriage, abortion, ectopic pregnancy, maternal death, neonatal death, and preterm birth.

(4) The number of prisoners who volunteered to participate in a substance abuse treatment program, and the number of prisoners who have participated in such a program.

(5) The number of prisoners provided medication-assisted treatment with medication approved by the Food and Drug Administration while in custody in order to treat sub- stance use disorder.

(6) The number of prisoners who were receiving medication-assisted treatment with medication approved by the Food and Drug Administration prior to the commencement of their term of imprisonment.

(7) The number of prisoners who

are the parent or guardian of a minor child.

(8) The number of prisoners who are single, married, or otherwise in a committed relationship.

(9) The number of prisoners who have not achieved a GED, high school diploma, or equivalent prior to entering prison.

(10) The number of prisoners who, during the previous year, received their GED or other equivalent certificate while incarcerated.

(11) The numbers of prisoners for whom English is a second language.

(12) The number of incidents, during the previous year, in which restraints were used on a female prisoner during pregnancy, labor, or postpartum recovery, as well as information relating to the type of restraints used, and the circumstances under which each incident occurred.

(13) The vacancy rate for medical

and healthcare staff positions, and average length of such a vacancy.

(14) The number of facilities that operated, at any time during the previous year, with- out at least 1 clinical nurse, certified paramedic, or licensed physician on site.

(15) The number of facilities that during the previous year were accredited by the American Correctional Association.

(16) The number and type of recidivism reduction partnerships described in section 3621(h)(5) of title 18, United States Code, as added by section 102(a) of this Act, entered into by each facility.

(17) The number of facilities with remote learning capabilities.

(18) The number of facilities that offer prisoners video conferencing.

(19) Any changes in costs related to legal phone calls and visits following

implementation of section 3632(d)(1) of title 18, United States Code, as added by section 101(a) of this Act.

(20) The number of aliens in prison during the previous year.

(21) For each Bureau of Prisons facility, the total number of violations that resulted in reductions in rewards, incentives, or time credits, the number of such violations for each category of violation, and the demographic breakdown of the prisoners who have received such reductions.

(22) The number of assaults on Bureau of Prisons staff by prisoners and the number of criminal prosecutions of prisoners for assaulting Bureau of Prisons staff.

(23) The capacity of each recidivism reduction program and productive activity to accommodate eligible inmates at each Bureau of Prisons facility.

(24) The number of volunteers who

were certified to volunteer in a Bureau of Prisons facility, broken down by level (level I and level II), and by each Bureau of Prisons facility.

(25) The number of prisoners enrolled in recidivism reduction programs and productive activities at each Bureau of Prisons facility, broken down by risk level and by program, and the number of those enrolled prisoners who successfully completed each program.

(26) The breakdown of prisoners classified at each risk level by demographic characteristics, including age, sex, race, and the length of the sentence imposed.

(b) Report to Judiciary committees.- Beginning not later than 1 year after the date of enactment of this Act, and annually thereafter for a period of 7 years, the Director of the Bureau of Justice Statistics shall submit a report containing the information described in paragraphs (1) through (26) of subsection (a) to the Committee on the Judiciary of the Senate and the Committee on the Judiciary of the House of Representatives.

SEC. 611. HEALTHCARE PRODUCTS.

(a) Availability.-The Director of the Bureau of Prisons shall make the healthcare products described in subsection (c) available to prisoners for free, in a quantity that is appropriate to the healthcare needs of each prisoner.

(b) Quality products.-The Director shall ensure that the healthcare products provided under this section conform with applicable industry standards.

(c) Products.-The healthcare products described in this subsection are tampons and sanitary napkins.

SEC. 612. Adult and juvenile collaboration programs.

Section 2991 of title I of the Omnibus Crime Control and Safe Streets Act of 1968 (34

U.S.C. 10651) is amended-

(1) in subsection (b)(4)-

(A) by striking subparagraph (D); and

(B) by redesignating subparagraph (E) as subparagraph (D);

(2) in subsection (e), by striking may use up to 3 percent and inserting shall use not less than 6 percent; and

(3) by amending subsection (g) to read as follows:

(g) Collaboration set aside.- The Attorney General shall use not less than 8 percent of funds appropriated to provide technical assistance to State and local governments receiving grants under this part to foster collaboration between such governments in furtherance of the purposes set forth in section 3 of the Mentally Ill Offender Treatment and Crime Reduction Act of 2004 **(34 U.S.C. 10651 note)**.

SEC. 613. JUVENILE SOLITARY CONFINEMENT.

(a) In general.-Chapter 403 of title 18, United States Code, is amended by adding at the end the following:

§ 5043. Juvenile solitary confinement

(a) Definitions.-In this section-

(1) the term 'covered juvenile' means-

(A) a juvenile who-

(i) is being proceeded against under this chapter for an alleged act of juvenile delinquency; or

(ii) has been adjudicated delinquent under this chapter; or

(B) a juvenile who is being proceeded against as an adult in a district court of the United States for an alleged criminal offense;

(2) the term 'juvenile facility' means any facility where covered juveniles are-

(A) committed pursuant to an adjudication of delinquency under this chapter; or

(B) detained prior to disposition or conviction; and

(3) the term 'room confinement' means the involuntary placement of a covered juvenile alone in a cell, room, or other area for any reason.

(b) Prohibition on room confinement in juvenile facilities.-

(1) IN GENERAL.-The use of room confinement at a juvenile facility for discipline, punishment, retaliation, or any reason other than

as a temporary response to a covered juvenile's behavior that poses a serious and immediate risk of physical harm to any individual, including the covered juvenile, is prohibited.

(2) JUVENILES POSING RISK OF HARM.-

(A) REQUIREMENT TO USE LEAST RESTRICTIVE TECHNIQUES.-

(i) IN GENERAL.- Before a staff member of a juvenile facility places a covered juvenile in room confinement, the staff member shall attempt to use less restrictive techniques, including-

(I) talking with the covered juvenile in an attempt to de-escalate the situation; and

(II) permitting a qualified mental health professional to talk to the covered juvenile.

(ii) EXPLANATION.- If, after attempting to use less restrictive techniques as required under clause (i), a staff member of a juvenile facility decides to place a covered juvenile in room confinement, the staff member shall first-

(I) explain to the covered juvenile the reasons for the room confinement; and

(II) inform the covered juvenile that release from room confinement will occur-

(aa) immediately when the covered juvenile regains self control, as described in subparagraph (B)(i); or

(bb) not later than after the

expiration of the time period described in subclause (I) or (II) of subparagraph (B)(ii), as applicable

(B) MAXIMUM PERIOD OF CONFINEMENT.-If a covered juvenile is placed in room confinement because the covered juvenile poses a serious and immediate risk of physical harm to himself or herself, or to others, the covered juvenile shall be released-

(i) immediately when the covered juvenile has sufficiently gained control so as to no longer engage in behavior that threatens serious and immediate risk of physical harm to himself or herself, or to others; or

(ii) if a covered juvenile does not sufficiently gain control as described in clause (i), not later than-

>(I) 3 hours after being placed in room confinement, in the case of a covered juvenile who poses a serious and immediate risk of physical harm to others; or

>(II) 30 minutes

after being placed in room confinement, in the case of a covered juvenile who poses a serious and immediate risk of physical harm only to himself or herself.

(C) RISK OF HARM AFTER MAXIMUM PERIOD OF CONFINEMENT.- If, after the applicable maximum period of confinement under subclause (I) or (II) of subparagraph (B) (ii) has expired, a covered juvenile continues to pose a serious and immediate risk of physical harm described in that subclause-

(i) the covered juvenile shall be transferred to another juvenile facility or internal location where services can be provided to the covered juvenile without relying on room confinement; or

(ii) if a qualified mental health professional believes the level of crisis service needed is not currently available, a staff member of the juvenile facility shall initiate a referral to a location that can meet the needs of the covered juvenile.

(D) SPIRIT AND PURPOSE.-The use of consecutive periods of room confinement to evade the spirit and purpose of this subsection shall be prohibited..

(b) Technical and conforming amendment.-The table of sections for chapter 403 of title 18, United States Code, is amended by adding at the end the following:

"5043. Juvenile solitary confinement."

© 2019 Federal Sentencing Alliance
www.FederalSentencingAlliance.com

Made in the USA
Las Vegas, NV
21 September 2023